TIBETAN FOLK TALES

TIBETAN
FOLK TALES

TRANSLATED BY

A. L. SHELTON, M.D.

(*Shelton of Tibet*)

EDITED WITH

AN INTRODUCTION BY

FLORA BEAL SHELTON

ILLUSTRATED BY

MILDRED BRYANT

GYAN

Published by

GYAN

Gyan Publishing House
5, Ansari Road
Daryaganj, New Delhi-110002
Phone: 011-47034999, 9811692060
E-mail: books@gyanbooks.com

Distribution Network
gyanbooks.com
India, USA, Canada, UK, Australia, France

ISBN : 978-81-212-9998-5 (PB)
First Published, 1925

2nd Impression 2021

Printed at: Gyan Press, Delhi.

Tibetan Flok Tales
Author: A. L. Shelton

TIBETAN FOLK TALES

TRANSLATED BY

A. L. SHELTON, M.D.
(*Shelton of Tibet*)

EDITED WITH
AN INTRODUCTION BY

FLORA BEAL SHELTON

ILLUSTRATED BY

MILDRED BRYANT

NEW YORK
GEORGE H. DORAN COMPANY

THE SEVEN SONS WHEN PLAYING IN THE FOREST FOUND
A BEAUTIFUL GIRL, WHO WAS HERDING A YAK.

The Story of the Two Devils

DEDICATED TO MY TWO
LITTLE GIRLS

DORRIS AND DOROTHY

WHO HAVE MADE SUN-
SHINE IN THE LAND
WHERE THESE TALES
WERE GLEANED

PREFACE

It is found among the old, old histories of the Tibetans that a female demon living among the mountains in Northern India mated with a monkey from the forests of Tibet, and from this union sprang the Tibetan race of people. The greater part of their literature is of a sacred nature, telling of their creation, of the formation of the world, of Buddha and his miraculous birth and death, of his reincarnations and the revisions of his teachings.

A kind of almanac, a little astronomy, plans for casting a horoscope, and many books filled with religious teachings and superstitions, including the worship of devils and demons, are about all that can be found.

The little stories in this book are told as the people sit around their boiling tea made over a three stone camp-fire. They are handed down from father to son, from mother to daughter, and though often filled with their superstitious beliefs, through them all run a vein of humor and the teachings of a moral truth which is quite unexpected.

These tales were gathered by Dr. A. L. Shelton on his trips among the Tibetans, around their camp-fires at night, and in their black tents high up in the mountains.

Every country has its folk-lore tales that have always been a joy and pleasure to the children, not only of their own land, but of other lands as well.

May these stories add a little to this pleasure and enjoyment everywhere, in whatsoever tongue they may be translated or in whatever land they may be read.

FLORA BEAL SHELTON.
(*Mrs. A. L. Shelton.*)

CONTENTS

Contents

ILLUSTRATIONS

TIBETAN FOLK TALES

ONE

The Wise Bat

If you are a parable unto yourself—there exists no evil.
Tibetan Proverb.

A LONG time ago, a *very* long time ago, when men and animals spoke to each other and understood the languages of one another, there lived a very powerful king. He lived far off in a corner of the world and alone ruled all the animals and men in his jurisdiction. Around his grounds and palace were great forests and in these forests many birds and animals lived. Every one seemed happy, except the king's wife, and she said that so many birds singing at the same time made such frightful discord that it worried her. One day she asked the king to call them all in and cut off their bills so they couldn't sing any more.

"All right," the king said. "We will do that in a few days."

Now, hanging under the eaves of the palace, close to the queen's room, was a little bat, and though he seemed to be asleep, he heard and understood everything the queen had said. He said to himself, "This is very bad indeed. I wonder what I can do to help all the birds."

The next day the king sent letters by runners into every corner of the kingdom, telling all the birds that by the third day at noon—and it mustn't be forgotten, so put this word down in the center of their hearts—that all of them were to assemble at the palace.

The bat heard the order, but because he was very wise and understood everything he sat very still thinking and thinking about what the queen had said and didn't go to the king's audience on the third day, but waited until the fourth. When he entered, the king said angrily:

"What do you mean by coming on the fourth day when I ordered every one to be here on the third day!" Oh, he was very angry indeed.

The bat replied, "All these birds have no business and can come whenever the king calls, but I have many affairs to look after. My father worked and I too must work. My duty is to keep the death rate from ever exceeding what it should be, in order to govern the sex question, by keeping the men and women of equal numbers."

The king, much surprised, said, "I never heard of all this business before. How does it come that you can do this?"

The bat answered, "I have to keep the day and night equal as well."

The king, more surprised, asked, "How do you do that? You must be a very busy and powerful subject to attend to all these matters. Please explain how you do it."

"Well," the bat replied, "when the nights are short I take a little off the morning, and when the nights are long I take a little off the evening and so keep the day and night equal. Besides, the people don't die fast enough. I have to make the lame and the blind to die at the proper time in order to keep the birth and death rate in proportion. Then sometimes there are more men than women, and some of these men say, 'Yes, yes,' to everything a woman asks them to do and think they must do everything a woman says. These men I just turn into women and so keep the sexes even."

The king understood very well what the bat meant, but didn't allow him to know it. He was very angry with himself because he had agreed to do so quickly what the queen had asked, and thought perhaps the bat might change him into a woman.

"I am not a good king," he thought, "when I listen to a woman's words and yield so easily, and I am terribly ashamed to have given this order. I'll just not do what my wife asks, but send these birds all back home and not cut off their bills."

So he called the birds all to him and said, "Heretofore, men haven't known how to mete out punishment and laws for you, but now I am going to make the Cuckoo your king, and what I called you up to-day for is this: I wanted to ask your King and the prime minister, the Hoopoe, to rule wisely, judge justly, and not oppress the people. If big or little come to you in a law-suit you must judge rightly between them and not favor either rich or poor. Now, you may all return to your homes."

But the king in his heart was still angry at the bat because he hadn't obeyed him and came the fourth day instead of the third, and to show him he was the ruler and to be instantly obeyed he gave him a light spanking for his disobedience and then turned him loose.

TWO

The Tiger and the Frog

The tall strong pine is a great help, for with its support the weak vine may climb as high.

Tibetan Proverb.

ONCE upon a time, in the days when the world was young and all animals understood each other's languages, an old, old tiger named Tsuden went out hunting for some food. As he was creeping quietly along the banks of a stream a frog saw him and was badly scared. He thought, "This tiger is coming to eat me up." He climbed up on a little bunch of sod and when the tiger came near, called out, "Hello, where are you going?"

The tiger answered, "I am going up into the forest to hunt something to eat. I haven't had any food for two or three days and I am very weak and hungry. I guess I'll eat you up. You're awfully small, but I can't find anything else. Who are you, anyway?"

The frog replied, swelling up as big as he could, "I am the king of the frogs. I can jump any distance and can do anything. Here's a river, let's see who can jump across."

The tiger answered, "All right," and as he crouched ready to jump, the frog slipped up and got hold of the end of his tail with his mouth, and when the tiger jumped he was thrown away up the bank across the river. After Tsuden got across he turned around and looked and looked into the river for the frog. But as the tiger turned, the frog let loose of his tail and said, "What are you looking for, old tiger, down there?"

The tiger whirled quickly, very much surprised to see the frog away up the bank behind him.

Said the frog, "Now I beat you in that test, let's try another. Suppose we both vomit." The tiger being empty could only throw up a little water, but the frog spit up some tiger hair. The tiger much astonished asked, "How do you happen to be able to do that?" The frog replied, "Oh, yesterday I killed a tiger and ate him, and these are just a few of the hairs that aren't yet digested."

The tiger began to think to himself, "He must be very strong. Yesterday he killed and ate a tiger, and now he has jumped farther than I did over the river. Guess I'd better slip away before he eats me." Then he sidled away a little piece, quickly turned and began to run away as fast as he could, up the mountain.

He met a fox coming down who asked, "What's the matter, why are you running away so fast?"

"Say," the old tiger said, "I met the king of all the frogs, who is very strong. Why, he has been eating tigers and he jumped across the river and landed farther up the bank than I did."

The fox laughed at him and said, "What, are you running away from that little frog? He is

THE FROG CLIMBED UP ON A LITTLE BUNCH OF SOD AND WHEN THE TIGER CAME NEAR, CALLED OUT: "HELLO, WHERE ARE YOU GOING?"

nothing at all. I am only a little fox, but I could put my foot on him and kill him."

The tiger answered, "I know what this frog can do, but if you think you can kill him, I'll go back with you. I am afraid you will get frightened and run away, however, so we must tie our tails together."

So they tied their tails fast in a lot of knots and went down to see the frog, who still sat on his piece of sod, looking as important as he could. He saw them coming and called out to the fox, "You're a great fox. You haven't paid your toll to the king to-day nor brought any meat either. Is that a dog you've got tied to your tail and are you bringing him for my dinner?"

Then the tiger was frightened, for he thought the fox was taking him to the king to be eaten. So he turned and ran and ran as fast as he could go, dragging the poor fox with him, and if they are not dead, they are still running to-day.

THREE

The Cony Who Got into Bad Company

If you are without kindness, you will meet no kindness in return.

Tibetan Proverb.

ONCE upon a time, a long, long time ago, when the world was young and new and the mountain tops were all peaks and the garden of Eden had not been pushed up towards the sky by the big high mountains of Central Tibet, men and animals understood each other. In a desert place, away among the mountains, was a little hut of mud and stone, and in this little hut with its dirt floor dwelt an old Lama. His house furnishings were very meager. There was a small piece of beaten felt upon which he slept at night and sat on cross-legged most of the day. He had no clothing and no covering at night except the one gown that he wore. He had some baskets of grain and sacks of tsamba, an earthen-ware pot for tea, and a small wooden bowl from which he ate. He dwelt in this house away from people that he might meditate and pray a good deal, and so acquire holiness. Every day he sat pondering the questions of life, and thinking about the little animals as well.

There was a cony by the name of Susha and a

rat by the name of Mukjong. These two were great friends and cronies, and both pretended to be friends with the old Lama, but at night when he was asleep for a little while, they would sneak into his hut and steal all the grain they could find. One day the Lama decided that these two were not really his friends, but were just pretending to be, and that they came to see him every day to discover what he had in the hut and then plan to come back at night and steal it. He said, "I'll just set a trap and catch them." So he fixed one of his round baskets into a little drop trap and that night caught them both. Next morning he found them, cut off their whiskers, ears and tails and turned them loose. They were very angry and said to him, "We belong to the Aberrang, and that is a class that doesn't lie, nor steal nor do any bad or dishonest thing. And you know we are your friends and have not stolen your stuff at all. We just wanted to see what you had in your basket and now see what you've done to us. Well, we're going to our own kings and ask them to send an army to take your grain for sure. So you better make a lot of traps to catch us all when we come."

The rat, very much ashamed of his condition, went to the king and showed him what had been done to him, telling him that he was innocent and asking that his king organize an army and attack the old Lama as a punishment for what had been done to him. The king, who was an old man, agreed to do so at once if the king of the conies would aid him. But when he asked the king of the conies he refused to help, as he knew the rat had been guilty. After the delegation had gone, the king of the conies called the cony to him, who came, looking very much ashamed, and told what had happened to him. The king said, "You only got what you deserved. When you are found in bad company you are judged as guilty as they. The rats are thieves and robbers and have been since the beginning of time, and when you are found with that kind of people you are thought to be just as bad as they. The conies are not a thieving folk, as you well know, and my advice to you is never to be found in the company of the rat or his kind of people again."

FOUR

The Story of the Donkey and the Rock

(A Black Tent Story)

Between iron and brass there is union if the welding is skillful.

Tibetan Proverb.

A VERY long time ago, somewhere in that far away land of Tibet, away up so high that it seems a little nearer the sky than any other land, in one corner was a country governed by a very just man. He was noted in all parts of the dominion for his fair judgment in all cases. In the city where this good king lived and had his home, dwelt two poor men. Both were very good, did the very best they could every day and each had an old mother to support.

One day one of the men started to a village high up in the mountains carrying a jar of oil, selling it as he went. Walking along, he grew very tired and set his jar of oil on a rock by the roadside while he sat down to rest a while. As he sat there, his neighbor came down the mountain driving his donkey in front of him. There were two big loads of wood stacked one on each side of the little donkey, which almost covered him. He didn't happen to see the jar, so came too near and knocked it off, breaking it, and spilling all the oil.

The man who owned the oil was very angry indeed, and the man who owned the donkey said it wasn't he who had done the damage, but the donkey. So they quarreled and quarreled and kept on quarreling. The man who owned the oil said he couldn't afford to lose it, as it was all he had in the world to sell for food for his mother and himself, and it couldn't have been his fault the jar was broken. They both went to the king who questioned them very carefully about the matter and finally said he couldn't see that either one was to blame. They were both good men, took good care of their old mothers and were honest in all their dealings, and so far as he could see no one was at fault but the donkey and the rock, and he would judge them. So the little donkey was chained with chains around his legs and around his neck and led into prison, while five of the king's men were sent out for the rock. As soon as they brought it in he ordered it wrapped with chains and tied outside the prison door to a post. By this time the news of this strange case and the queer doings of the king had spread throughout the city. When the people heard their great king was having a trial about a donkey and a rock they thought he had surely gone mad. The next morning the king announced by his runners through the city that the case would be tried. The idea that a donkey and a rock could have a trial in court was more than the people could understand, but early next day everybody in the city was at the courtyard to see

THE DONKEY, ALMOST COVERED WITH THE LOAD OF WOOD, DID NOT SEE THE JAR, AND BROKE IT, SPILLING ALL THE OIL.

the result of the trial. When the time arrived the judge came, took his seat, instructed the door-keepers to shut and lock all the gates, thus locking in everybody, and then proceeded to pronounce his judgment on the case.

"As you very well know, there is no law by which a donkey and a rock can be judged. Why have you all come to see so absurd a thing? Now, because of your curiosity in the matter, every one of you shall pay a half-cent before he gets out."

The people, looking much ashamed, and glad to get out, handed over this bit of money and slipped through the gate. The cash taken in this way was given to the man who had lost his oil, so he was happy, the debt was paid, and the court closed.

FIVE

Story of the Foolish Head-Man

Do not brag of your family—without fame they may be—the strain on the string of an arrow soon makes it useless. The horse traveling fast comes to the end of his strength very quickly.

Tibetan Proverb.

ONCE upon a time, away among the mountains, were located two little villages. One was called Jangdo and the other Jangmeh. One head-man ruled over these two villages. He was a very wise man, but had an only son who was foolish, with a wife that was very wise. After a while the old man died, and his place had to be filled by the son, who was an idiot. A river ran alongside of the village and a takin died and fell into the water. The upper village claimed it and the lower village claimed it, so both villages came with the request that it belonged to them.

His wife said to him, "Now you do not know to which place this animal belongs, but you must go and decide about it. Decide in this way: say that the upper half above the ribs belongs to the upper village and the lower part belongs to the lower village and the middle part is yours because you are a middle man." He did as his wife said, and when the people heard this decision they thought, "Why, we have always thought this man to be foolish, but he is a very wise man," and his fame spread abroad.

After two or three months had passed, a leopard died and floated down the river, stopping in the same place as the takin, and the villagers quarreled again. Only this time they did not want it, so the upper village said, It is yours, and the lower village said, It is yours. They finally took it to the head-man, who thought to himself, "I will not ask my wife this time, I will do it myself. I know how it ought to be done and I will do it just as I did the takin." So he divided it just as he had done before. But one village said, "Well, we don't want this part," and the other village said, "We don't want ours either." So they gave it all to the head-man, who put it all on a horse and took it home. His reputation for wisdom was done and the people said he had turned again into a foolish man.

SIX

How the Fox Fell a Victim to His Own Deceit

Between the official and his people is confidence if the head-man is skillful.

Tibetan Proverb.

ONCE upon a time, away up in the corner of the mountains, in a little cave, lived a tiger and her baby cub. She had brought for this baby, one day when she was out hunting, a little fox to be his playmate. The fox had a happy time and an easy one, for he didn't have to work or hunt, but played all day and the mother tiger kept them all supplied with food. One day she went out to hunt and found a little calf, which she took home to be another playmate for her son. But the fox was much displeased and became very jealous of the calf because he thought they all loved the calf better than he and that only the food that was left over was given to him. As a matter of fact, they treated him just the same as ever, but his heart was wrong and he began to plan how he might be revenged on the calf. After a while, the mother tiger became very ill, and as she was about to die she called the calf and her son to her side and said, "Although you are not of the same father and mother, yet you are brothers. I don't want you to ever quarrel, but to live happily here together, and if any one should tell you lies don't pay any attention to them, but always be friends." So saying, she died.

Now the fox saw his opportunity. Every morning the calf was in the habit of running and playing and jumping and shaking his horns in fun, bellowing and taking exercise, while the tiger preferred to lie and rest. So one morning while the calf was skipping around, the fox slipped up to the tiger and said, "Although the calf says he is your friend, have you any idea what he is thinking about, when he runs and jumps and shakes his horns in that manner? In his heart he hates you, and in that manner is gaining strength in order that he may be able to kill you."

This, of course, made the tiger suspicious and very angry. So daily he watched the calf very closely and became sour and surly.

Then the fox went to the calf and said, "You know your mother told you and the tiger that you were to be brothers, but see, he is growing larger and stronger every day and his heart has changed and he is preparing to kill and eat you."

The tiger and the calf were now enemies and watched each other with a great deal of suspicion and were very unhappy. Finally one day the calf said to the tiger, "Why do you want to kill me and eat me? I have done you no harm and love you just as your mother said I should."

The tiger replied, "I love you just the same and

never thought of doing such a thing until the fox said you were preparing to kill me."

Then they realized that the fox had been trying to make them enemies, and they decided on a plan to get even with the fox. The tiger said, "I'll tell you what we'll do. We'll have a sham fight saying we hate each other and we're going to fight it out and see who wins. Ask him to be present and while we're in the midst of it, I'll attack him."

The day came and they began their fight. They maneuvered round and round and seemed to be fighting very fiercely until they came very near the fox, when the tiger made a jump, landed on him and killed him and sat down and had a feast of the carcass.

This shows what happens to those who try to make trouble between friends.

SEVEN

The Ingratitude of Man

Whatever you have promised make it not as changeable as a loop in a string, but as firm as a line on a rock.

Tibetan Proverb.

ONCE upon a time in a far, far away land, in a very high, high land, when the old world was very, very young and animals and men spoke and lived together, such a thing as gratitude was known.

Away in the mountains was a narrow road that passed along the side of a deep chasm. It was a dangerous place to travel, and along this path one night, just at dark, when a man, a crow, a rat and a snake were walking along together, a part of the road gave way and they fell into the depths below. They were not hurt, but much shaken, and they sat there waiting and thinking of their plight, wondering how they could get out, or what they could do to keep from starving, when a traveler coming along reached the broken road and looked down and saw them. They all at one time began to clamor and beg to be helped out, so he threw a long rope down to them and drew them all out one after the other. They all professed great gratitude and said they would never forget him and never forget the help he had given them, and that some time they'd help him. The traveler, in his heart, rather scorned the professions of friendship from the crow, the rat and the snake, and really didn't believe they could do anything for him, but thought possibly the man might be able to aid him some time.

A long time after this had taken place, in the palace of the king, in this far away country, the queen was on the top of the flat roof washing her hair. She took off her jeweled necklace and laid it down near her on a low bench, and when her hair was dry went downstairs and forgot her jewels. Near by in the top of a tree sat the crow who had been rescued by the man a long time ago. He saw the necklace and said, "This will be a good present to give to that man who saved me from the chasm," so he flew down, picked it up in his bill, flew away with it and took it to the man and told him where he got it.

The next day the traveler with the necklace met the man he had rescued and said, "Look here. I didn't think that crow would be much of a friend, but see, he has brought me these magnificent jewels that belong to the queen."

The rescued man, hearing this, went at once to the king and said to him, "The queen's necklace you will find in the house of such a man," and gave the name of his rescuer. The king at once sent his men, arrested the traveler and cast him into prison. In that dark old dungeon, with no bed to lie on, the walls dripping moisture, no food to eat, and no friend to bring him any, he

IN THAT DARK OLD DUNGEON, WITH NO BED TO LIE ON, NO FOOD TO EAT, IN THE COLD AND DAMP, HE WAS ABOUT TO STARVE, WHEN THE RAT HE HAD RESCUED CAME AND ASKED HIM HOW HE HAPPENED TO BE IN THAT PLACE.

was about to starve to death, when the rat he had rescued and who lived there came and asked him how he happened to be in that place. He related the story of his arrest and the ingratitude of the man he had saved and said he was about to starve and would surely die unless help came very soon. The rat went away, entered into the king's palace, stole the food from his table, carried it to the man in the dungeon and saved him.

Another day the snake came in to see him and asked how it was that he happened to be in the prison. He told him the story again and the snake said, "Never mind, I'll get you free."

Now this snake was a magic snake, and making himself into a ghost wound around and around the king's neck and almost choked him to death. He could be felt but not seen. The king wildly called for his great men, his wise men and his lamas who cast lots and told him that this ghost that was choking him was one of the patron saints of the man in the prison, and if he would loose the prisoner and treat him kindly, his troubles would cease. So he called for the prisoner to be brought before him, gave him much money and many jewels and sent him away speedily.

The king's misery stopped and the traveler was made happy by the friendship of the three whom he had doubted and scorned.

EIGHT

Covetousness

As hail leads rain—so a quarrel leads relatives apart.
Tibetan Proverb.

LONG ago, hidden in a deep valley in the mountains, was a pool where all the animals went to drink. Near the pool was a road, and across the road a hunter had set a big bow that would shoot a long spear into whatever animal loosed the taut string. A bear coming along tripped over the string, the spear was loosed and it killed him instantly. A fox came along and said, "Ah, here is enough meat to last me a year, but I guess I had better cut the string that holds the bow, for fear the hunter will return and set it again for me."

So he chewed it and the bow sprang, striking him on the head and killing him instantly. Near the place where the two lay dead was a gully, and in it lay an elephant asleep. A rabbit came along and saw the elephant lying still, played and hopped around, until finally the elephant opened his eyes and watched him.

"That's very queer that a little fellow like you can jump so far. I believe I'll try it," he thought. So he gave a big jump and his front feet caught and loosed a big rock that fell on his back and killed him. All three were dead now, the bear, the fox and the elephant. Then seven robbers came along and exclaimed, "Just look at the meat, we will stay here a few days and eat." But they must have water too, and nobody wanted to carry it. Each wanted the other to go. They finally got three to go and the four who were left said, "We will fix up three nice pieces of meat and put some poison in it for them when they get back, and we four will have all this meat, bones and ivory." So they fixed up the poison meat for the three men who were gone, for they had to go a long way over the mountain after the water. The three who carried the water said: "Those four fellows are bad men, we are doing all the work carrying this water for them, so we will put some poison in it, then we can have all the meat." When they got back the others were very thirsty and took a big drink, and in a little while they were all dead. "Now," said the three, "we will have all this meat and stuff ourselves." So the three took meat already cut and ate that, and in a little bit they were dead too.

Now the moral is, "First, people shouldn't be greedy when there is plenty for all (the fox wanted all the meat to eat for a year and tried to ruin the bow and got killed). Second, you mustn't do what you aren't fitted for (the elephant tried to do what the rabbit was doing and got killed). Then the four men begrudged the three and the three begrudged the four, so they all died.

NINE

The Wise Carpenter

For men there is no hope—except to find happiness in the worship of the gods.

Tibetan Proverb.

ONCE upon a time in the city which was called Snalong lived a King whose name was Gendong. This King died and his son, Genchog, ruled in his stead. Among the people under him were two men, one a painter, who did exceedingly fine work, the other a carpenter, who was also of the best, and these two men were enemies. One day the painter came up to the new King and said, "Last night as I was ready to go to sleep, your father sent an angel out of Heaven to call me, and I went to Heaven with him to see what your father wanted and found him rich beyond belief. He gave me a letter to bring to you, and here it is; this letter is about that fine carpenter that dwells here in this city."

The King opened the letter and read: "My son, I am here in Heaven, very wealthy, and I have all that I want except one thing, and that is I wish to build a Hläkäng, or temple, to the gods. But there are no good carpenters here and I want you to send me up the best one in the city. The painter who brings this to you knows all that I mean, for he has been here, and I'm sending the letter by him."

So the King, Genchog, said, "This must be my father's letter, for it is like him to want to build a temple to the gods, and I must see to his wishes at once." So he called the carpenter before him and told him, "My father is in the dwelling of the gods, is very happy, but wants to build a Hläkäng and asked me to send you up to help him."

The carpenter thought it queer that such a thing could occur, and said to himself, "It must be a scheme of that painter to get rid of me. I must think of some plan to get ahead of him." Then he said, "Läso, [which means so-be-it] but how am I to get there?" Then the King called the painter and asked him how he was to send the carpenter to his father. The painter said, "This is the way. He is to bring all his tools that he will need up there, put them on a pile on the ground, sit on them, then wood must be piled around him and set on fire. As the smoke goes up, he can ride on it to Heaven." "Well, that's all right," said the carpenter, "but I want to start from my own field." The King gave him seven days to get ready. The carpenter went back home to his wife and said, "That painter has fixed a scheme to kill me, and I have only seven days to wait to be burned up, so we must work, for I want a tunnel dug from my house out to the field where the burning is to take place." They got it done and put a few sticks over the opening where he could pile his tools and sit on them. The

King, as soon as the seven days were up, ordered his people to bring several loads of wood, each to carry a load and a bowl of oil. So the wood was piled four square around the carpenter, the oil poured on and set on fire. While the fire was big the carpenter slipped down in the tunnel. The painter exclaimed, "Look, there he goes, riding the smoke to Heaven." They all took it for the truth and went home.

Now, the carpenter had a dark secret room in his house and in there he stayed, washing himself every day and having some clothes made like the gods wear. At the end of three months, putting on these garments, and with skin as white as a lily, he came out of his house and went to see the King, bearing a letter to him from his father. Thus read the letter, "My dear son Genchog, it is said that you are a good ruler and rule your people wisely and well. Some three months ago you sent me a carpenter to build a Hläkäng, and he has finished it beautifully, and I want you to see that he has his reward on earth when he comes back. Now that the temple is done I want the best painter that you have in the kingdom to come and paint it for me. The same plan that you chose in sending the carpenter will do very well for sending the painter." The carpenter told him how rich his father was and of his adventures in the sky. The King gave him great riches, making him happy for life. And after reading the letter the King sent for the painter and said, "The carpenter has just come down from Heaven, and has brought a letter asking you to come and paint the Hläkäng for my father." The painter looking at the carpenter, with his skin so white, dressed in such strange clothes, with strings of coral about his neck, while he was still in his old clothes, thought perhaps that it was all right to go to Heaven that way, and half believed that the carpenter had really been there. So he got all of his things together; as he had been given seven days to prepare, the wood and oil had been brought with some things which the King wished to send to his father. When all was ready the carpenter said that they must make music for him as he ascended. So they got drums, horns and cymbals, and as the fire started began to beat loudly and made a great noise. As soon as the fire reached the painter he yelled that he was being burned up, but the noise was so great he couldn't be heard, so he really did go to Heaven.

TEN

The Story of Drashup and the Goddesses

In birth and death there is no fear, and in fear there is no doubt.

Tibetan Proverb.

ONCE, long ago, in this land of mystery, where men lived and loved and wondered and died, lived a man named Drashup, who was all alone in the world. All his kin were dead. He had no wife, no children, and he was very, very poor. One day he wandered away upon the mountain and lay down and went to sleep, grieving over his troubles.

Just at this time, in a small village far below at the foot of the mountain, a little girl was born. In the tree under which the man was lying asleep dwelt a goddess. All around him in the wood dwelt a number of goddesses, and it was their duty to cast lots and foretell this new little lady's future: who her husband would be, when she was to be married, if she would live to be old, and the day of her death. The goddess who lived in the tree under which Drashup was sleeping invited all the others to come to her tree, as she had a guest asleep near her dwelling. So they came and began to forecast the lady's future:—She would

ONE DAY HE WANDERED AWAY UPON THE MOUNTAIN AND LAY DOWN AND WENT TO SLEEP, GRIEVING OVER HIS TROUBLES.

be only middle-aged when she would die from eating the shoulder of a sheep and the man asleep under the tree was to be her husband.

The man was not very sound asleep and overheard all these predictions, which made him very angry, and he said, "Such talk! It is all foolishness. I'm a middle-aged man now and the very idea that I'm to be the husband of a baby just born."

But nevertheless he started out to hunt this child. He traveled and traveled up and down the country, and finally found in the village at the foot of the mountain, a little girl who had been born on that very day, and he knew that it was she about whom they had been speaking. So he slipped quietly up by the side of the house, picked up a small ax used to chop firewood, slipped around where the girl was and struck her. Believing he had killed her he ran away into a far country; but she recovered and grew to womanhood.

By and by the girl's parents died and she was left an orphan with nothing at all, so she left her home and went traveling. By chance she went to the city where Drashup had taken up his residence. They met one day and instantly fell in love. As he was talking to her one time, he saw a big scar on her head and asked her how it came to be there.

"My parents told me that one time a man named Drashup took an ax and tried to kill me, in the village where I was born," she told him.

When Drashup heard this, he knew there was no use to try to get away from the words of the future foretold by the goddesses of the mountain, but he didn't tell her how she was to die, though he remembered that, also.

They were married and lived happily, though he was so much older than she. But he was always very careful to take the shoulder of the mutton for himself and see that she never got any of it. She, however, wondered why he always wanted the shoulder for himself, and one day when he was absent from home on business she killed a sheep and said, "As Drashup isn't here I'll eat the shoulder myself." After eating it she remarked, "It was awfully good, no wonder he always wanted it himself." Then suddenly she became violently ill and Drashup found her dead when he came home, and knew for sure that never could any one get away from the decision of the goddesses.

ELEVEN

How the Louse Got the Black Streak Down His Back

Eating pleasant things is like listening to words of praise.
Tibetan Proverb.

ONCE upon a time in this wonderful land where we dwell, where the sky is so blue and the mountains so high and the clouds so white and soft and woolly and so very close to the earth, here it was animals and men worked and struggled and spoke together.

At the foot of a great mountain one day a louse and a flea were preparing to go up into the timber and carry down a load of wood. Each had his rawhide strap with which to tie on his load, but before they left, knowing they would be hungry, they stood up three stones and put a big pot of soup and flour and meat upon them; then built a fire under it, leaving it to simmer until they should return, agreeing that whoever came down first with his load could eat it all up.

The flea was sure he would get home first because he could jump so far, but he found every time he jumped his load of wood slipped and some of his sticks fell out and he had to stop and replace and retie it. The louse plodded slowly along, but kept going steadily, so he got there first and ate up the pot of food. When the flea arrived, he was as angry as could be and said, "You've eaten all the food," and grabbing the empty black kettle threw it at the louse, who dodged the blow by turning his back, and the kettle struck him squarely in the middle where it left a long black streak from the soot on the outside of the pot.

So to-day you can see that mark down the back of a louse if you will take the trouble to catch him and look.

TWELVE

The Man and the Ghost

As you desire the sun, so you desire your friend's return.
Tibetan Proverb.

ONCE upon a time a man was walking along a narrow mountain path, when he met a ghost. The ghost turned around at once and walked along beside him. The man was very much frightened, but didn't care to let the ghost know it. Pretty soon they came to a river which had to be crossed, and as there was no bridge or boat both had to swim it. The man, of course, made a good deal of noise, splashing and paddling the water, while the ghost made none at all.

Said the ghost to the man: "How does it happen that you make so much noise in the water?"

The man answered, "Oh, I am a ghost and have a right to make all the noise I want to."

"Well," the ghost replied, "suppose we two become good friends, and if I can help you I will, and if you can ever aid me you will do so."

The man agreed, and as they walked along the ghost asked him what he feared more than anything else in the world. The man said he wasn't afraid of anything he saw, though inwardly quaking all the while. Then he asked the ghost what he was afraid of. "Of nothing at all," said the ghost, "but the wind as it blows through the tall-headed barley fields."

By and by they came near a city, and the ghost said he was going in to town. But the man said he was tired and that he would lie down and sleep a while in the barley field at the edge of the city. The ghost went on into town and played havoc, as ghosts generally do. He proceeded to steal the soul of the king's son and tying it up in a yak hair sack carried it out to the edge of the barley field where the man lay asleep, and called out to him, "Here is the soul of the king's son in this bag. I'll leave it here for a while and you can take care of it for me, as I have a little business elsewhere."

So saying, he put the sack down and went away. The man now disguised himself as a holy lama, begging tsamba, and, carrying his prayer wheel and the sack, started for the city. When he arrived he heard at once that the king's son was about to die and he knew what was the matter with him. So he went to the palace begging and the king's chamberlain said to him, "You are a very holy man, perhaps you can do something to help the king's son get well." The man said he would try if they would let him in to see the king.

When the king saw him he said, "If you will heal my son, I'll give you half of all I have, lands, gold, cattle and everything." So the man said he would. He took his yak hair sack, sat down on the ground, cross-legged, as all Buddhists sit, made a little idol of tsamba meal, opened the sack and thrust it in, allowing the soul to escape. Then

THE MAN NOW DISGUISED HIMSELF AS A HOLY LAMA, BEGGING TSAMBA, AND, CARRYING HIS PRAYER WHEEL AND THE SACK, STARTED FOR THE CITY.

he tied the mouth of the bag with nine knots, blew his breath upon it, said many charms and prayers over it, and while he talked, lo, they brought the king word that the boy was recovering. The father was so pleased and happy, he kept his word and gave the man half of all he possessed. The ghost never, so the story goes, came back or claimed the sack he had left with the man, and the man thought, "Perhaps that is the customary etiquette between a man and a ghost."

THIRTEEN

The Wicked Stepmother

Eating much the tiger can swallow no more, so the vulture may safely come down.

Tibetan Proverb.

ONCE upon a time, on the very tiptop of a big flat mountain, there was situated a country over which ruled a king named Genchog. He married a beautiful wife who gave him one son whom they named Nyema. In giving birth to him she died, but the baby lived. The king got him another wife and had another son whom they called Däwä. One day, thinking to herself, she said, "There is no chance for my son to be king, for the older son has the birthright and he is sure to be the ruler."

So she began to plan and plot and see if she could think of some way to kill the older son and let her son rule the kingdom.

One day she feigned to be very ill and rolled over on the floor groaning and crying. The king saw her and very much alarmed exclaimed, "What is the matter with you?" And she answered, "Oh, I have had this sickness since I was a little girl, but it has never been so hard as it is this time. There is a way to cure it, but it is too hard and bitter, so I will have to die this time."

The king asked, "What is the way to heal you? I don't want you to die, for it would break my heart and I wouldn't want to be king any longer. You must tell me the remedy so I can save you."

She demurred for some time but finally said, "Well, one of your sons must be killed and I must eat his heart with butter, but you see your older son is the prince and heir to the throne and the younger son is my own flesh and blood, so I could not eat his heart even if it were to save my life."

The king was dreadfully grieved and finally said, "Well, I love one son as much as another and my heart would ache the same for each of them, but in a day or two I will kill the elder, as it would do no good to kill the younger."

After a while the younger brother found out what was to be done and went to the older brother and told him, and asked, "What shall we do about it?" The older brother said, "Little brother, you must stay with your father and become the king. He won't kill you and I'll run away." The younger brother felt very sorry about it and his heart was sore as he said, "If you are going away I want to go too. I don't want to stay here without you." "Very well," answered the other, "you may go if you wish." So they arranged together to slip away that night at midnight and tell nobody of their going. They could take no tsamba for fear some one would find out they were going. They had some tsamba bags and in them were some dried tsamba tormas that the lamas had been using. Now these tormas are little cone-shaped bodies made of tsamba and are used when the lamas are reading prayers. They are supposed to be full of devils, which the lamas coaxed into them when they read their holy books.

They started about midnight on the fifteenth of the month and traveled day and night, over the mountains and through the valleys, until their dried tsamba was all gone and they were very hungry and thirsty. They finally came to a village, but there was no water. The younger was getting weak now as they had had but little food and no water for some time. So Nyema said to him, "Wait and rest here in this little village, and I will go and see if I can find some water." He kept on going until he had gone entirely around the mountain in his search for water, but found none. Going back to the place where he had left his younger brother, he saw that he was dead. He was very much grieved and built a tomb for him of prayer stones and prayed that in his next incarnation he would have a happy life and not have to have so much sorrow as he had had this time. Nyema then left and, crossing two mountain ranges, came to a cliff in which was a big door through which he entered, and there found an old hermit lama in the cave. When the old man saw him he said, "You are a good man, I know by looking at you. How did you happen to come here?" Then Nyema told all that had happened to him and why he had run away from home, so the old man said, "You can stay here and be my son and I will pray to the gods to bring your younger brother to life again." In a few days the younger brother did come to life, and following his older brother's tracks came to the old hermit's house, and the two stayed there as the old lama's sons.

Below this cave, which was high up on the mountain, was a city where dwelt a very good king, and near the city was a big lake by which all the people watered their fields. Every year an offering had to be made to the snake god who dwelt in the lake, so that he wouldn't be angry and keep the water away. For this offering the people must sacrifice a human being who had been born in the tiger year. But the time came when all the people born in this year were dead and gone, and none was left to offer. One day the children, seeing the king, said to him, "Every day when we go up on the mountain to herd the cattle, we see a lama who lives up there. This lama has two sons, and the older one was born in the tiger year." So the king sent three men to see if it was true. The men went up to the cave and knocked on the door. The lama opened it and asked, "What do you want?"

"The king has heard you have two sons and that one was born in the tiger year," answered the men, "and we need him for the offering to the god of the lake."

The lama answered, "I am a lama, how could I have two sons?" Then he shut the door in their faces and hid the boys in a big water cask. This treatment angered the men so they took some rocks and beat the door down. They looked everywhere for the boys, but they were so carefully hidden they couldn't be found, so in their disappointment they took some rocks and beat the old man. The boys couldn't stand this, so they came out of their hiding place and called, "Here we are, don't beat him any more." Then the men tied the older son and took him with them to the king. The lama and the younger brother felt very sad after he was gone. The men led Nyema to the king's palace, and since it wasn't quite time for the offering to be made, he was allowed his freedom in the courtyard of the palace. The king had a daughter, who fell violently in love with Nyema when she saw how handsome he was, and watched him wherever he went.

The day finally came and they took Nyema to the lake to throw him in. The king's daughter followed, saying pleadingly, "Please don't throw him into the lake, but if you must, throw me in too."

It made the king angry to see his daughter act in that manner, and he called out, "Throw her in too." So they threw them both in. Nyema felt very sad and he thought, "It doesn't matter if I am thrown in, as I was born in the tiger year and the people will all starve if the snake god is angry, but it seems useless that the princess should die on my account." The girl thought to herself, "I am only a girl and it doesn't matter if they do throw me in, but it is too bad to kill this handsome young man."

The god that ruled the lake thought it would be a pity that since they loved each other so much either should die, so when they were thrown into the water he carried them to the shore and neither of them was drowned. Then the god told the people it wasn't necessary to sacrifice any more, that he would see that there was plenty of water without it.

Nyema said to the princess, "You go to your father and tell him what the snake god says. I want to go see the lama and my brother for a little while. In a few days I will return and we will be married."

The princess went back to the palace, and Nyema to the cave. When he knocked on the door a faint voice answered, and when he opened the door the old lama said weakly, "I had two sons, but the king took one away from me to sacrifice to the snake god and now myself and my other son are about to die."

Nyema said, "This is your son returned." Then he washed and fed them and they were soon better and very happy to have him with them again.

When the princess returned to the palace every one was glad to see her and rejoiced. Her father asked her if Nyema was dead and she answered, "No, and it is because of his goodness that I live. The snake god doesn't want any more human sacrifices of the tiger year nor any other year, and the water will always come and will never be stopped."

The king and his head-men thought it miraculous that they had been saved and that the god of the lake had been so kind. The king then ordered Nyema to be brought before him. So they sent messengers and this time invited the three to come down the mountain, and when they arrived the king set them on high benches to give them honor.

Then he said to Nyema, "You are a worker of wonders, are you really a son of this old hermit? Nyema answered, "No, I am the son of King Genchog. My brother and I ran away from the kingdom and from my father's wife, who was not my real mother, to save our lives." So the king, knowing him to be the son of a king, was much pleased to give him his daughter in marriage. Not only his daughter did he give him, but his scepter as well, and let him rule in his stead, for he was growing old.

Then Nyema made a feast for all the people and gave them a happy time for a period of seven days. When he had mounted the throne one day he said to Däwä, "Little brother, you must go back home and see your father and mother, as it has been a long time since we left them." The new king gave his brother jewels and gold and silver, and then decided they would all go. They took yak loads of goods, many presents, all their servants and the two sons with the princess, started on their way. About half way over the big mountains they wrote a letter and sent it on ahead by a runner, telling their father they were coming. When the father heard his two sons were still alive he was very happy and sent out people to meet them. When he had welcomed them and found his older son had a kingdom, he turned his crown over to the younger son, which was just what the mother wanted. After a visit the older son took his princess and went back to his kingdom, where the two ruled long and well and lived happily ever afterwards.

FOURTEEN

The Story of the Two Devils

The golden eagle flying high you are not able to bind, and great water running swiftly you are not able to dam.

Tibetan Proverb.

A LONG time ago in a country so high that it would make most boys and girls tired if they tried to run and play, was a great flat table-land entirely surrounded by a forest. On this table-land was located one large city and several smaller ones, all ruled over by a king who had seven sons. The sons went out in the forest to play one day and found a beautiful girl, who was herding a yak. She told them she was the daughter of the King of the west, that their yak had wandered away and she had come to hunt it. The seven sons thought that she was very pretty to look at, so they proposed to her that she become the wife of the seven, which was the custom of the country. Now, in reality, the girl was a she-devil and the yak was her husband. They could change their form whenever they chose. She didn't tell the men that the yak was her husband, but drove it away and consented to become the wife of the brothers and went home with them.

Every year one of the sons died, beginning with the eldest, until all were dead except the youngest, and he became very ill and was about to die. The head-men of the villages got together and wondered and wondered what could be done, shaking their heads and muttering that this was a very queer affair, that these six sons, whom they had cared for and to whom they had given all the medicine they knew of, had all died. They thought the matter over and decided to send for a man who they knew could tell fortunes, and see if he could discover what was the matter. Four men were chosen to go and see him. They traveled until they found him, told him all about the death of the six brothers, and asked him to cast lots and see what was the matter. He told them that he would lie down and sleep and receive a vision on the affair and to-morrow would relate it. Actually he didn't know what in the world to do nor what to say, for he was not a really-truly fortune teller at all, but only a quack. That night he went to ask his wife what to do, and she said, "You've told a lot of lies about things before this, so it won't hurt you to lie some more. You came out fairly well the other times, so I think that you can fix up a plan for this affair."

The next morning when the four men came, he said, "My vision was fine, I will get out my black clothes and black hat and read prayers for you. We will all go back together and these charms that I read will make everything all right in the palace."

So he took a big rosary in one hand and the skull of a hog in the other and traveled along with them. When they arrived the woman didn't know exactly what to think, and wondered if this fellow really did know her and her husband and what they had done. The fortune teller made a tsamba torma and placed it at the head of the sick man, along with the hog's skull, and covered them both with a cloth. When the she-devil left the room the sick man got a little better and went to sleep. This scared the fortune teller so badly he didn't know what to do. He thought the man was dying. Really the man's soul had been about half eaten up before the woman left, and when she went away it grew stronger. The fortune teller was badly scared and called out two or three times for help and began to think he had better step out and take his things and run off, but the door was locked and he couldn't get it open. He wondered if he could hide some place until he had a chance to slip away, so he sneaked upstairs to the top of the roof and fell through the opening in the dark, astride the yak's horns, and the yak went bucking and tearing away with him on its head.

The she-devil was down there too, because she was afraid. The yak called out, "This man knows us all right, for he lit right on top of my head and knows I am the he-devil, for his charm is in his hand and he is beating me to death with it. What shall I do?"

His wife replied, "He knows me and I dare not come over and help you; and just as sure as can be in the morning he will call all the people together, and they will be planning some scheme to get rid of us."

They thought in their hearts that perhaps he would call all the women to carry wood and burn them in the fire, or kill them in some other dreadful way.

"Truly," she said, "to try and find out if we are real they will hit us with rocks to see if it will hurt, and cut us open to see what is inside of us and put us in the fire to see if it will burn us."

The man in the meantime had rolled off the yak and heard all this, so he knew now what to do. Slipping back upstairs he set up his tsamba torma and hog's skull and began to read prayers again.

The King's son was awake by this time and the fortune teller asked him if he wasn't better and he said "Yes."

"Well then," the man said, "in the morning you must call your head-men together, have them tell all the people to bring their guns and swords and some of the women to bring wood."

The next morning they were all there with the wood piled around the center as if for an offering to an idol, as the fortune teller had commanded them. He asked that his saddle be put on the yak. He donned his black clothes and rode the yak all over the city until he came to the pile of wood. He now grabbed his hog's head and hit the yak three times saying, "I want to see the real body of this yak," and the yak turned at once into a he-devil with a hideous face, two of his upper teeth hanging down to his breast and two lower ones extending up to his forehead. The men standing around killed him with their swords and guns. Then the fortune teller called for the woman to come. She came screaming, and he struck her with the hog's skull and she turned into a terrible thing, with a most ugly face, clawlike hands, a great long tongue and teeth like her husband's. The people killed her with rocks and knives and burned them both in the fire; then hastened to do great honor to the fortune teller, who had gone back to the sick man.

The King's son got well right away and was so pleased he said to the fortune teller, "Whatever you wish, ask, and I will give you."

"Well," said the fortune teller, "I would like some of those wooden rings that are used to lead the yak around by their noses." (The reason he wanted them was because his wife always said he couldn't make them properly.) So the son gave him one hundred rings and enough goods to make seven yak loads and he returned to his home.

His wife saw him coming, took some wine and went to meet him. That night she asked him all about his adventures and he told her about the death of the two devils and the recovery of the King's son.

"And is this all you have, some dried cheese and meat and a few rings for the yak?" she said, and scolded him soundly. "To-morrow I will go and see the King's son." But she wrote a letter instead which said, "You have given my husband this little bit of stuff and the nose rings which can have but one meaning, which is, that perhaps your disease may return."

When the King's son received the letter he said, "That is all true. I gave him all he asked for, but perhaps I should have given him more." So the next day he went to visit the fortune teller and said to him, "You have saved my life and done so much for me, now I will make you ruler of half my kingdom." So he made him as powerful as himself.

FIFTEEN

The Wise Woman

Either going up or down a ladder it is an evil thing if you are pushed.

Tibetan Proverb.

A LONG, long time ago there were two countries adjoining each other and one was a little smaller than the other. The king of the farther and bigger country was named Gezongongdu, and the king of the smaller country was named Drashi. The king of the larger country thought he would like to make the smaller country subject to himself. "But first," he said, "I want to see if their king is very wily and wise. If he isn't I can conquer him; but if he is, I shall not attempt it."

He took a mare and a colt that were exactly alike in color and size and asked the king to decide which was mare and which was colt. The head-men came first and looked and looked and couldn't tell at all. One of them went home and told his wife and she said, "That's easy, I'll tell you how to do it. You make a manger and put some grass in it for them. The mother will keep pushing the food over toward the colt." Sure enough it happened as she said it would, so they were able to answer the king's first riddle.

The next day the king sent a stick shaped the same at both ends and asked them to tell which was the top and which the root. The men all came and looked and looked again, but couldn't tell. The same head-man told his wife and she said, "That's easy, throw it into the water and the head will go down stream first and the root will come last." They did so and the problem was solved for the king that day.

Then the king of the larger country sent over two snakes, male and female, and none of the wise men could tell them apart. The head-man again went to his wife and she said, "That's easy, take a piece of silk and place it near them, the female will think it is nice and soft and she will lie down on it, curl up and go to sleep; but the male will run away and refuse to sleep." They did that and it all came true just as she said.

So the king of the big country decided he didn't want to fight the king of the small country, for he was too smart. But the little king knew he had been saved from war and called up his head-man and asked him how he had got all these things right when everybody else had failed. He answered that he didn't know anything about these things, it was his wife. So the king called the head-man's wife and gave her many gifts and made her husband chief head-man of his kingdom.

SIXTEEN

The Three Friends

The man who agrees with every one and has no opinion of his own is like a horse who with a bridle is driven in every direction.

Tibetan Proverb.

ONCE, a long, long time ago, in a little mud village tucked in between the mountains, there lived three friends. Two of them were very rich, but one was poor. Nearly every week they went out to have a jolly time and always took food along with them and spent the day playing in the woods and talking together. The two that were rich always carried the lunch, but the poor one never brought anything at all. He was the biggest eater of the lot and would finish about everything left over from what the others had brought with them. So the two began to think of a scheme that just once they might get ahead of him.

One day, fixing up their lunch bags, they slipped away from him and followed the river around the mountain until they came to a nice shady place well hidden among the trees, and there decided to have their dinner and a good time without the other man. He hunted and hunted, but couldn't find them, and said, "They didn't tell me the truth to-day as to where they were going and I can't find them, but I expect they have gone down the river." So he said to his sister, "You get me a box quick, bring it here and put me in it and shove it out into the stream, and I'll float down the river and come to the place where they are hiding. They'll see the big box and think they have found something worth while, and will pull me out."

Sure enough, in about an hour, the rich men saw the big box come floating down and were very much excited. They got a rope, threw it over the box and drew it to the bank.

"I expect we have found something great," one of them said, and could hardly wait until, with stones and knives, they had the board off the top; but when they found the man they were running away from they were as angry as could be.

The poor man said, "What in the world did you pull me out for? Heretofore I have always eaten your food and had nothing to bring, until I was so ashamed I decided to drown myself and got in this box to do it. Now it's just my luck that you pulled me out. You have saved my life, so bring your food and I will help you eat it up. It is your own fault, for you pulled me out of the water; so we will eat good and full." He proceeded to do so, and as everything was finished, he remarked, "Well, when you have anything good to eat another time, just tell me about it and I won't trouble you to pull me out of the water again."

SEVENTEEN

The Rabbit and Bumblebee Bet

An empty-handed official has no chance, neither will a wet vine cause the tea to boil.

Tibetan Proverb.

ONE day a rabbit was sitting by the side of the road under a bunch of nice grass, and near him sat a bumblebee on a big yellow flower. As they sat talking together they made a bet; the rabbit saying, "I can swell up bigger than you can," the bumblebee replying, "You can not." So they decided to try. The rabbit swelled and swelled, and some one passing said, "Look at that rabbit, he looks as big as a wolf." Then the bumblebee puffed and puffed until some one passing said, "Look at that bumblebee, he looks as big as a yak;" so he won the bet.

EIGHTEEN

How the Rabbit Killed the Lion

To your foe do not give a promise, for he carries a sword.

Tibetan Proverb.

A LONG, long time ago, before the mountains were melted, and the trees were burned, and the animals all died, the sun was so hot that the mountains all ran down level with the plains. Then the king of beasts on the earth was the lion, and every morning all the animals had to come and kotow to him. One day there was a rabbit in a nice soft bed of grass, feeling so comfortable that he didn't want to go and kotow to the king. He didn't see any use of it, didn't know exactly where the lion was, and he was having too good a time anyway. All of a sudden the king stood before him looking like a thunder cloud. He spoke and said, "You little split-nosed rascal, here you are having a nice time eating grass, and have not come to kotow to me. All the other animals have made obeisance this morning. You do not value your life at all, do you?"

The rabbit thought, "If I don't tell this lion a lot of big lies, he will surely kill me, so I must tell them to save myself." Very politely, he said, "This morning when I got up to go to make my obeisance to you, I came to a stream of water, and in it was a big she-devil and I was afraid, and ran up here a few minutes ago to hide in this grass."

The lion asked, "Did that devil harm you?"

"No," answered the rabbit, "she didn't hurt me, she only yelled as I went by and my heart seemed as if it would break into two pieces, and that was enough for me. She asked, 'You little short-footed fellow, where are you going so fast?' I answered, 'I'm going to make my obeisance to the king of beasts.' Then she said, 'Well, we are going to see about that, son, and find out who is greater, he or I. I've hunted every place for this lion and can't find him, so when you go to kotow to him, you tell him for me, that I want him to come here where I am in this water, and we will see who is to be the ruler of the beasts.' So if you have anything to say to her I'll go take the message, as it would not do for you to go down there."

The lion answered, "I haven't anything to tell you, but I have something to say to that devil, and I'll go down and say it myself. There isn't anything on earth or any devil that can be bigger or think themselves bigger than I am, or more able to rule the beasts, for I'm the biggest there is. If she whips me, I'll be the same as a dog and let her rule."

The rabbit thought, "I'm in for it now, I'll lead him down and let him see for himself." He led him to the stream, and when the lion saw his re-

THE KING OF THE BEASTS AT THIS TIME WAS A LION AND EVERY MORNING ALL THE ANIMALS HAD TO COME AND KOTOW TO HIM.

flection his hair all bristled up and his tail lashed from side to side. The rabbit, dancing up and down, yelled, "There she is, there she is." Whereupon the lion flew into a great rage, jumped into the water to fight and drowned himself.

NINETEEN

How the King Lost His Great Jewel

During the dark of the moon the robber can steal the yak's calf.

Tibetan Proverb.

ONCE upon a time there was a king who had a great diamond which he admired very much; he liked to let the sun shine on it and see it sparkle. But he had some servants who were very dishonest and who decided to rob him of the jewel. So that there would be no suspicion attached to them, the servants decided that they would make the jewel disappear while the king was looking at it. It was the king's custom to have it taken out in the light so that he might see all the colors of the rainbow in it. This day he took the jewel out and placed it quite a distance away, and as he looked at it, it shone and shone, but the sparks seemed to get less and less and it finally disappeared before his eyes. He and his servants went to look for it but they could find nothing, because they had used a piece of ice to deceive him. The king lost his great jewel; it had vanished before his eyes, and the blame could be placed upon no one.

TWENTY

The Story of the Three Hunters

Be the work good or bad, we cannot tell what may be said of it, nor how far its result may spread.

Tibetan Proverb.

ONCE upon a time, when the world was young and men loved and hated as they do now, in a mountain village there lived three brothers and they were hunters. Each of the brothers had married a wife, and they had one sister who lived with them all. One day they went out to hunt and brought in a deer. When they had all the meat they wanted to eat they gave a leg bone to the sister, who cracked it, took out the marrow and toasted it, so that it looked very good. As she sat eating this delicacy, the wives of the two elder brothers became very angry, just why it would be difficult to say. They were so angry that they decided they would plan some way to kill the sister. They said, "The brothers think so much of her that they won't consider us at all, so we must get her out of the way."

Again the brothers all went out for a hunt, and the women decided now was the time. The wife of the younger brother would have nothing to do with it and told them it was the wrong thing to do, because the sister had had only her share of the meat. But the wives of the two older brothers decided to kill her anyway. When the brothers were coming home they stopped on the way to rest and a little bird in a tree kept singing and singing the same tune over and over. Finally one of them said, "That bird seems to want to say something to us, I'm going to see if it does, for it sounds like my sister." He went up to the tree where the little bird sat and said, "If you are my sister, hop up on my hand." The little bird hopped on his hand and they all began to cry, because they knew their sister was dead. They went on home and found the three wives, but the sister was gone. They said nothing about her being away, but later they found the younger wife crying and she wouldn't tell why. They told her they knew why, as they had seen the sister, and her soul had gone into a bird. So the young wife told them the story, and they were so angry that they killed the two big wives and had the third in partnership.

HE WENT UP TO THE TREE WHERE THE LITTLE BIRD SAT AND SAID, "IF YOU ARE MY SISTER, HOP ON MY HAND." WHEN THE LITTLE BIRD HOPPED ONTO HIS HAND, THEY BEGAN TO CRY, AS THEY KNEW THEIR SISTER WAS DEAD.

TWENTY-ONE

The Hunter and the Unicorn

An old Lama without religion and a heart without happiness hurt very much. *Tibetan Proverb.*

ONCE, long ago when men's hearts were evil and they forgot to be grateful for kindness, a hunter was walking along the road and fell over a cliff, almost killing himself. As he was wondering how he could get to the road again, a unicorn came along, stopped and looked over at him. The man began to beg and plead, saying, "You are such a nice unicorn. I have never harmed any animal, except when I was hunting and hungry, and I never would hurt you." He begged and coaxed until the unicorn came down and helped him up on the road again. When he was safely out he said, "Now I know the road out of here, so I have no more use for you." He grabbed his gun and shot the unicorn dead. Sure enough, it was a bad road and he wandered around and around, but could find no end, no way out, and wished he had asked the unicorn the right road before he had killed him. Finally growing tired and weak and hungry, and no one coming to help him, he fell down the cliff again and died.

Moral: Don't be sure you know more than you do.

TWENTY-TWO

The Decision of the Official as to Who Owned the One Hundred Ounces of Silver

When the official is avaricious there is much talk—when a poor man eats meat and wine it is the same.

Tibetan Proverb.

ONCE upon a time, in a tiny hut on the side of a mountain, there lived an old wood-cutter who was blind, but who had a dutiful son who cared for him very well. The son went upon the mountain one day to bring in his load of wood, and as he was carrying it on his back down the steep path, he found a little leather bag, in which were ten pieces of ten-ounce silver chunks. This was a great fortune and meant ease for himself and his father all the rest of their lives. He hurried home, and when his father asked him how he had fared that day he answered, "Fine. I've just found a bag of silver, and we won't tell anybody about it at all." But the father said, "No, we must be honest. Bring it here and let me see it, and then take it up to the head-man of the village and tell him all about it." The old man took it out of the sack, felt it all over and put it back again, and then bade his son take it to the official.

One day a man came walking in and said he had lost his bag of silver. The official thought he could find it for him and sent for the young fellow to bring him the bag, but when the man found he was going to get his money back so easily he said to himself he would claim a little more. He told the official he had twenty pieces in the bag and the boy had stolen ten of them. The head-man quietly said to one of his servants, "You go down and hear the blind man's story of the affair and come back and tell me what he says."

Then, when the servant returned he said the old man's story was the same as the boy had told. The man who had claimed the silver stood waiting, expecting to have the ten pieces and ten more added to it as well. The official said, "This silver belongs to the boy, this is not yours. Yours had twenty pieces and this has only ten. You will have to look elsewhere for yours and I will let the boy keep this to help him in the support of his old father."

TWENTY-THREE

Story of the Prince's Friend

A man without jewels in the mountain has no need to fear the robbers.

Tibetan Proverb.

AWAY, away up in the mountains was a village, and in the village lived a very wise king and his only son. Near by flowed a river; up above was a big pond from which came the water that irrigated their fields, and above the pond, in a crevice from which flowed the water, lived two big frogs, who belonged to the lower regions. To these frogs, every year, some person had to be sacrificed or the supply of water was cut off by them as they sat in the crevice, through which the supply came. Each family in turn had paid its tax of a child, until now it was the turn of the king to furnish the yearly sacrifice. So the old king began to think and wonder which had better go—he or his son—each one thinking he should be the one. The father said, "I'm an old man, and if I go and get eaten up it doesn't matter, for I wouldn't live much longer anyway. So, my son, when I'm gone you must be a good ruler and govern the people wisely."

The prince said to his father, "This will never

do; you are a good king to these people and you can get another wife and have more sons, so don't say any more about it, for I'm going."

One morning he started for the place. All the people went with him a little way and felt very bad to see him leave them and his father. After a while all of them returned home except one friend of his childhood, who still went on with him, crying and grieving. The prince now turned to him and said, "You must go back and be a good son to your father and care for him when he is old." But his friend replied, "When I was a child and poor you cared for me, fed me and clothed me, now you must not go and let those frogs eat you up. I'll go in your place."

The prince would hear of no such plan, however, and as his friend refused to return, they both went on together and arrived at the mouth of the gorge where they saw one green frog and one yellow frog sitting together talking. The yellow one said to the green one, "Here comes the prince and his friend, and if they are wise they would take a clod and kill us, then they would have all the water they needed, and whenever they wished they could vomit gold and jewels. But they don't understand frog talk, so they don't know what we are saying." But the king's son did understand, for in those days all kings and their sons understood what the animals said. So he told his friend and they each got a club, killed and ate the frogs, and plenty of water came through the crevices.

"Well," the friend said, "now these frogs are eaten and out of the way, let's go home."

But the prince said, "No, it would be better if we go to a far country, as the people think we are eaten by those frogs, and if we return now, they will think we are ghosts and fear us exceedingly."

So they crossed the mountain and went down on the other side, where they came to a wine shop kept by a woman and her daughter, and went in.

"Bring out your wine," they said, "we wish to buy some. How much do you ask for it?" When brought they vomited a few jewels which they gave as pay for it.

The two women, when they saw how they got their money for the wine, said, "Drink some more, drink some more," thinking that if they got them real drunk they would throw up a lot of gold. They were soon very sick sure enough and threw up gold and jewels all over the room, and the woman and the girl got more than enough to make them wealthy.

When they began to sober up, they feared they had thrown up a lot of jewels, but were a bit ashamed to ask about it, as they weren't sure what they had done.

So they went on, coming to a big plain where a lot of children were playing. They were quarreling over something, each claiming it to be his. The travelers asked what they were quarreling about and the children replied, "We found a hat and whoever puts it on can't be seen, for he turns into a ghost, and we all want it."

The prince's friend said, "You needn't quarrel over that; you children all go down there and race up here to me; the one who gets to me first may have the hat. I will hold it."

Soon they came racing back, but the man put the hat on his head and when they arrived they could not find him or the hat, though they searched everywhere and finally had to go home without it. When they were gone the man removed the hat and put it in his bosom. He and the prince then went on and came to a place where a lot of monkeys were quarreling, and when they asked what they were fussing about, they answered: "We found a pair of boots, and whoever puts them on has only to wish where he wants to go and he will be there at once, so we all want them."

The prince's friend said, "Well, don't quarrel; give them to me and you all go and run a race, and the one who wins can have them. In the meantime, I'll hold the boots."

As soon as they were gone he jerked the hat out of his gown, put it on his head, and when they got back he wasn't to be seen. They hunted every place, but could not find him, and finally went away without their boots.

Then the prince and his friend put on a boot each, and the prince wished to find a place where the king was dead, where they wanted a new ruler; and they both went to sleep. Next morning they awakened to find themselves in the midst of a great hollow tree, and around it was a crowd of men who that day were to choose a new king.

While they stood there they prayed that the god of the sky would throw down a tsamba torma from the clouds and hit whoever was to be the king. So down it came, but instead of hitting any of them it hit the big tree. "This won't do at all," they said, "we haven't any such custom as having a tree for a king." But an old man was there who said, "Let's see if some one isn't in the tree." They looked and found the prince and his friend inside. But the people were not at all pleased.

"This will not do at all," they said, "we don't know these men, we don't know their fathers and mothers and they are probably bad men. We won't have them now, but to-morrow we will have another test and whoever can vomit the most valuable things, he shall be king."

The next day one drank a lot of milk and threw up white every place he went, another ate something green and threw up green, and others different things. The prince vomited gold and said, "You see, I am to be king." The friend of the prince vomited jewels, and said, "You see, I am to be the prime minister." So they were made king and prime minister of the country.

The prince found a beautiful girl, whom he took to be his queen. Now the prince had two houses, one very high on the mountains and another in the city, and every day the queen went up to this high house for a little while, but he did not know she went there. However, his friend did, and wondered and wondered why she went up to that house every day. "Somebody or something must be in there that she wants to see," he thought. So he put on his magic hat and went along behind her when she started for the mountain. She went in through an open door, up a flight of stairs, through another door, and up another flight, and so on for five stories, until she reached the top of the house, which was beautifully fixed with rugs and hangings. She took off her everyday clothes and bathed and perfumed and gowned herself in silks and satins and lit incense. The prince's friend was sitting by, invisible of course! After two or three hours a beautiful bird flew down from heaven. The queen lighted a piece of incense and went before the bird with it, as it had perched itself on a rock near her on the top of the house. It really was the son of a god, disguised as a bird, with only feathers or bird's clothing on the outside. She fixed food for him, and he stepped out of his bird gown, and as he held her hands he said to her, "Your husband was chosen by the gods to be the king; is he a good or a bad ruler?"

The queen answered, "I'm very young, and whether he is good or bad I'm unable to say."

Then they said good-by and she asked him to come again to-morrow morning. So he flew away in his bird gown and she donned her everyday clothes and went back to the palace.

Next morning it was the same thing, the minister of the king accompanying her, invisible again.

The god said to her, "I'm coming to-morrow in

the king's palace as a bird and see for myself whether the king is good and wise and whether or not he is handsome."

Next day, before the queen came, the prime minister told the king all about his lady, that she went to this high house on the mountain every day to meet the son of a god, and that he had put on his invisible hat and gone along and had seen them, while they could not see him, and he knew all about it.

"So to-morrow," he said, "you make a big fire of charcoal on a 'hopan' and take a sword and kill him."

They were all sitting around a big fire next morning, the king, the prime minister and the court, when the bird came hopping up the stairs into the midst of them. The minister had on his hat and couldn't be seen; he grabbed the bird by the tail, threw some fire on him and the king took his big sword to kill him, when the queen caught his arm and would not allow him to do it. The fire burned the bird on the back and wings a bit and he flew very quietly into heaven again. The next day the queen went again to the high castle, and dressed once more in her beautiful clothes, and again the minister went. She waited a long time and felt dreadfully sad about the whole affair, but that day the bird did not come. One day after this he came flying down very slowly, for he was covered with burns and felt very ill. The queen took his hand and cried over him.

"You need not cry," he said, "the king is a very

good and handsome man, but it is very queer he should throw fire all over me. I am very sick these days with all these burns and can not fly very well, and will only come once a month to see you, not every day." And he flew slowly away.

The queen went back to her king and began to love him better, because the son of the god came only once a month to see her.

The prime minister one day put on his magic hat and his boots and wished himself back where he had drunk wine in the inn with the woman and her daughter. On the way he passed the door of a small lamasery and slipped up and looked in, where he saw two old men, caretakers of the place, drawing a donkey on a piece of paper; as they turned the paper over one of the men turned into a donkey, got up and rolled over and ran all over the lamasery, braying in a dreadful manner. It seemed that the drawing turned one way, changed the man into a donkey, and turned over, changed him back into a man. When the old man was tired of his queer piece of paper and the tricks it did, he rolled it up and put it behind the big idol. The prince's friend, who had his magic hat on so that the old priest could not see him, slipped in and stole the paper, then went on to the wine shop and said, "I want to pay you for the wine you gave us; here is five tenths of an ounce of silver, and I will give you a paper, which, if you turn it over, it will bring you plenty of gold." They said they would be very glad to have it if they could get hold of wealth that easily. So he gave them the paper, and as soon as they turned it over, they both turned into donkeys. Then he led them to the king who used them to carry wood and dirt to fix his houses, and they were half starved and were very bad off indeed. After working and carrying for three years they were very ill and their backs were terribly sore.

One day the king saw them with the tears rolling down their faces, and he asked, "What is the matter with these donkeys; why are they crying? Turn them out and don't make them work so hard;" but the minister had the paper and turned them back by turning the paper over and they returned to their homes. Then he told the king he had punished them for the way they had been treated so long ago.

TWENTY-FOUR

How the Raven Saved the Hunter *

For a foolish official to speak skillful words is as difficult as for lightning to split a lump of bronze.

Tibetan Proverb.

ONCE upon a time there was a very poor man with nothing much to eat and very little to wear, who made his living by hunting. One day he went out to hunt and traveled and traveled up hill and down. At last he came to the top of a mountain, hungry, tired and thirsty, as he had had nothing to eat all day. He stood still a few minutes thinking and wondering what he would do. Looking around he saw a valley far below with a cold stream of water flowing through it. Starting down, he made him a cup of a leaf as he went, came to the stream, dipped his leaf full and started to drink it. Just as he was ready to swallow it a big raven flew by and with his wing struck the cup from his hands. The hunter thought it was an accident, so dipped another drink, when the old raven knocked it from his hand again.

Then he began to be angry at the bird, when he dipped the third time and the raven knocked this out of his hand. He said angrily, "All right, I'll

* Perhaps a variation of the same story told of Genghis Khan.

fix you," drew his bow and shot the raven dead. When the bird was dead the man began to wonder why he didn't want him to drink the water. "Perhaps I had better not drink now, but I'll go to the head of the stream and see where the water comes from." He went a short distance and found that the stream issued from the mouth of a great snake, and looking along the banks he saw many skeletons of birds and animals that had been drinking the water. Then he grieved greatly because he had killed the raven that had tried to save his life.

TWENTY-FIVE

The Two Thieves. (A Black Tent Story)

In the presence of a kind man you are uncomfortable, in the presence of bad food there is an odor.

Tibetan Proverb.

THERE was once upon a time two thieves, one named Lozong, the other Adra. They went out one day and slipping down the mountain stole one of a herd of cattle that belonged to a rich man. They drove this cow into a ravine and killed it where nobody could see them. They were afraid to leave the beef and go and wash the stomach and intestines, as each was afraid the other would run away with it. Adra wanted to stay with the big beef, so finally after much persuasion Lozong took the intestines down to wash them. And both were afraid the rich man would discover what they had done. As Lozong washed and washed and cleaned the intestines he wondered how he could cheat Adra out of his part of the beef. Adra sat and schemed how he could cheat Lozong out of his part. But Lozong had the best plan. He took the stomach and blew it up as big and tight as he could, got him a club and began to beat it as if it were a big drum, all the time yelling. When Adra heard him he was very much frightened and said, "A kä kä, they have caught him now, and are giving him a good beating; they would have gotten me if I had gone down there to wash those things, so I will run away as fast as I can and they will think that he was the only man that did the stealing." So he ran away as fast as he could, and when Lozong got back he kept all the beef himself and laughed to think how easily he had won it from the other thief.

TWENTY-SIX

The Golden Squash. (A Black Tent Story)

The shepherd will protect his flock of sheep and without power can save a hundred lives.

Tibetan Proverb.

ONE time in a corner of the world, high up among the mountains, there lived two old men who were very good friends. Each had a small garden patch. One was a good old man, naturally; that is, he didn't have to try very hard to be good, for his heart was pure, he loved all animals and birds and was very happy in his little garden. But the other old man wanted very much to be wealthy. One day the first old man found in his garden a little, crippled bird. He took it and cared for it, felt sorry for it, healed it and fed it every day. Then he was able to fly away, and the old man let him go. He soon returned bearing a seed in his mouth which he gave to the old man, saying, "You plant this seed—it's a very fine squash seed, the very finest in the world, and be sure you tend it well."

So the old man planted it and watered it, and at last there grew on the vine just one squash, but it was monstrous big. When cold weather came and it was fully ripe the old man tried to pull it and take it into the house, but he couldn't carry it and had to call five men to help him get it in. By and by he wanted to eat some and peeled off the outer skin, which was very thin like paper, and when he cleaned it, he found it to be solid gold. Now, he was very rich, but he made good use of his money and gave to the poor and aided all who were needy. His old neighbor came over one day and asked him where he got the seed for that squash, and he told him the story of the little bird. The old man went home, very envious, and thought he would think up a plan so that he would be rich too.

He got his bow and arrow and slipped out into the garden and waited until he saw a little bird light on a tree. Then he deliberately shot, breaking its leg. Picking it up carefully, he pretended to be grieved over its hurt and tended the little thing until it was finally well and able to fly away. One day sure enough the bird flew back bringing a seed which he told the man how to plant and care for because it was very wonderful indeed. It sprouted and grew and grew until finally when winter came he had to have five or six men help him carry his squash into the house. He was much delighted, for he thought, "Now I shall be rich, too." He could hardly wait until he could get his knife and cut the skin, but he had no more than broken it when it popped wide open and out jumped a fierce old man, who said he was sent by the king of the lower regions to weigh him. He grabbed him by the back of

THE BIRD RETURNED BEARING A SEED IN HIS MOUTH, WHICH HE GAVE TO THE OLD MAN.

the neck and set him on the scale which he carried and said, "You are far too light and no use at all," and at once took him out and cut off his head.

So much for the sin of covetousness.

TWENTY-SEVEN

The Story of the Bald-Headed Man

Eating much of sweetness you do not know if it be sweet any more. But the evil in a man shows and you know it very well.

Tibetan Proverb.

ONE time, when the world was young and men and women were ill because an evil spirit possessed them, there lived a man and his wife who were very poor. A devil came and took possession of each of them and made them both sick. As they were not rich they couldn't invite a holy lama to read prayers for them, so invited a lay-brother in his stead. After a while this man who was reading began to get very hungry. It was the custom to give the priests the best of food, but this man and his wife had no butter nor meat nor fine things to eat. They had no horses, nor yak and only one goat. So the reader began to think to himself that if they would kill this goat he'd have plenty to eat, as it was really pretty fat. The man who owned the house was bald-headed and now he came up and sat on the roof near where the man was reading. He really sat down in front of him and heard the man mumbling his prayers, "Om mani padme hum, Om mani padme hum;" he was reading, and read right on in the same tone, "The god says if a man is bald-headed and will take the skin of a goat and put it on his head he will have hair." The old man sat and heard him read this over several times and finally decided it was there in the book of prayers; so he killed the goat. They all had some good eating for a while and the old man put the skin on his head, wore it and wore it for days and days and kept feeling his head, but not a single hair would come. He finally concluded that the man had lied to him out of the book, and besides, he thought, "If I wear this too long, I fear all the skin will be worn off my head and there will be nothing but bone." So he asked the man about it, whether he hadn't lied to him, and he said, "Oh, no, but if a man would have what the gods say come true, he must pray a great deal himself." Thus he got around his lies and had goat to eat as well.

TWENTY-EIGHT

The Man with Five Friends with Different Colored Eyes

(A Black Tent Story)

A man who can succeed is always sent—if there is nothing to be done, it doesn't matter who goes.

Tibetan Proverb.

ONE time there was a man who had a son. The man was not wealthy and hadn't much to leave his son, but he said there were just two things he wanted to tell him before he died; if he heeded them he would be happy, if he didn't he would be very miserable. The two things were these: first, when you are married never trust your wife with your secrets until you have ten children; second: choose your friends by their eyes. "Never choose for a friend a man with a light colored eye," he said, "see that the inner corner of the eye is red and that the white of the eye is pure white and not brownish or yellow, and that the colored part is black. Now, if you will observe these two things you will never get into trouble."

After his father's death he soon married, and as he was a very amiable man, made many friends. It happened that one of his friends had blue eyes, one yellow eyes, another brown eyes, another black, and only one came up to the father's stipulations. He heeded his father's warning about telling his wife his secrets until after his first son was born, then he was so pleased and so happy, he told her what his father had said, but remarked, "I believe you will be trustworthy though, so I will tell you some of my secrets." But he was a bit doubtful still, and resolved to put her to the test.

One night, coming home late, he stopped at a man's place and bargained for a hog for twenty rupees, and the man was to tell nobody to whom he had sold the hog or where it had gone. He took the hog, killed it, drew off his trousers and put the hog in them, threw it over his back and carried it home. When he got there he called his wife in a loud whisper, saying, "Let me in, let me in quick."

"Why, what is the matter?" she asked.

"I've killed a man, let us put him in the pond."

So she helped him and they tied rocks to the trousers and sank it in the water. The man was all covered with blood, carrying the dead pig. He went in and washed himself, taking off his soiled clothes, saying to his wife, "You must never tell this to anybody, for it is as much as my life is worth if you do."

One day he and his wife had a quarrel.

"You treat me this way, will you," she said, "I'll show you what about yourself. You know that man you killed, well, I'll tell the official about it." And she did. He sent an officer to come and get the man and put him in chains until the time should come for his beheading.

The man sent word now to his five friends. All came and listened to his tale, and four of them said, "Well, you did this, you told your wife you did, and you will have to take the consequences, for we can't help you." Then the four left. His last friend came and after hearing his story said, "This is terrible. I don't know what I can do, but I will save you if I can."

So he went up to the official and told him that his friend had been a very good man and must have been greatly provoked to kill any one, so, if he would spare him, he would give him the man's weight in silver. The official finally consented, had the silver weighed and the man was released. The friend who had helped him was very happy and the man seemed happy too. He turned to the official and said, "May I tell you a good story, one of the best you ever heard?" His friends were all standing near and heard him relate what his father had told him before he died, how he resolved to test it, and how his wife at their first disagreement had told on him to the official, and how his friends had all deserted him but the one whose eyes were as his father said they should be.

The official said, "You are one of the wisest men I ever heard of," and sent men to take up the corpse of the pig, proving his tale to be true, and was so pleased with him that he gave him many presents and made him one of the chief men in all his realm.

TWENTY-NINE

The Story of the Violinist

When the robber arrives it is very difficult for the traveler to string his bow and carry tea and wine at the same time.

Tibetan Proverb.

IN a great city, a long time ago, lived a family composed of the father, the mother and three sons. As they grew up and were ready to take up an occupation, the father called them to him and said, "I want you all to go out into the world, each to a different place, and learn a trade." All of them went, and after a year's time came back.

The father said to the oldest, "What have you become?" "Oh, I am a writer," and the father was well pleased, for now he would have some one to keep accounts and look after his business affairs.

To the second one he said, "And what have you learned?" He answered, "I am a carpenter;" and again the father was pleased, because he could build their homes and build the homes of other people, and so make much money.

Then turning to the youngest, "And what have you become?" he asked. "Oh, I have learned to play the violin," he answered. "Oh, very good indeed, you have learned a beggar's trade and can stay with me no longer, so you must leave."

So the third son went to a far country, even as far as the shores of the white men, where bounding their country was one black sea. Here he played his violin. In that place dwelt two snakes, a black one and a white one, and one day they began to fight. The black snake was about to kill the white one when the fiddler parted them. Days went by, when one evening an old white-haired woman came and said to the musician, "The king of the lower regions is greatly indebted to you, as you have saved his son, and if you will go to this lower kingdom the king will give you whatever you want and desire the most."

He said, "I don't know how to go to the lower regions, how do you get there, anyway?"

She told him it was not difficult at all. "But if you will shut your eyes, I will carry you, and you will be there in a little while. When you arrive you ask for whatever you desire most." She told him that the daughter of the king was very beautiful, and because she was so pretty she covered her face and body with the skin of a chicken so she could not be seen.

Then the old woman said, "Don't ask for very much, but tell the king if he will give you a hen you will be satisfied, for if you get the daughter of the king you get a very dear treasure, and obtaining her, you can get anything else you want."

Now the old woman picked him up, he closed his eyes, and soon they arrived at the lower kingdom. The king said, "You saved the life of my son, so I am very much indebted to you. Anything in the world you want, that I will give you." The violinist replied, "There is nothing I want very much, but there is a hen over there you might give me." The king answered, "That is all the daughter I have and I love her very much, but I can't say I won't give her to you, for that would be breaking my word. Daughter, you must go, follow this man up into the hills when a lucky day comes, and if there is anything I have that would be of use to you, I will give it to you to take when you go."

The daughter said, "Whatever my father says, that I will do. I would not dare disobey. I do not want to carry much away, but please give me three things. I want a golden pick, a gold chain as long as I can reach from one hand to the other, and a brass blessing cup (put on the head by the lamas in blessing one). Also, I would like a jar of fruit, a lot of feathers, a few of many kinds of hair; these things I will take."

Then these two, the musician and the daughter of the king, on the first lucky day ascended to the earth and went to a city where ruled a very wicked monarch.

Now the wife of the fiddler had great power within herself, and whatever she wanted came to her, so they did not have to do any work at all. One day the musician thought thus in his heart, "We two are very rich now and are second to the king himself in power, and perhaps if this wicked ruler discovers that we are so wealthy he would take all our belongings. I'm going to make a feast to the king, invite him to eat it and see if he so purposes in his heart."

He asked his wife if she thought it would do. "Well," she said, "if you invite the king and give him a feast, when he comes you must be sure to give him the things very quietly, the wine and the good things to eat, but do not be slow in the serving." So the king was invited, and all went well. As the fiddler was a man who liked to be flattered a bit and who wanted to be very polite to the king, he kept saying, "Stay a bit longer, stay a bit longer." His wife, because it was so hot, as they had had a charcoal fire for a long time cooking the feast, threw off her garment of feathers. It seemed as if the house got brighter when she had done this and the king, seeing how pretty she was, wanted her for his wife, and said to the fiddler, "We are going to trade wives," and took her away with him.

After a few days the king called his chamberlains and head-men from different parts of the province and said, "There is a man here who has given me the daughter of the king of the lower regions for my wife. Now heretofore you have not done much work and what you have done has been very poor. There is a mountain standing over on that side of the country and you are to level it even with the plain, making all the land equal in height."

His servants all answered, "If you will demand another thing we will do it, but this we are not able to do. Suppose you call the former husband of this woman and tell him what is required." So he called the musician and said, "Can you do this?" He answered, "Yes," without thinking, "I can make this level for you." When his wife heard him say this, she waited for him near the stairs, and when he came she said to him, "You know the gold pick I brought with me that my father gave us. You take that and strike the mountain three times on three sides and it will disappear."

The king and his stolen wife went out to see it done, and lo, as he struck the third time the mountain sank and a pond stood in its place.

When the king saw his work he said, "Well, if you can do this you can do a bit more. Where this pond is, make a big lake. On the borders I want the finest of trees bearing luscious fruit, full of singing birds and many animals in among the trees."

The violinist did not know how in the world he could accomplish all this, but thought he would slip around and ask his former wife how to do it. She said, "Take that blessing cup and pour some water from it into the pond and it will become a lake. Take seeds from the fruit we brought and plant on the edge of the lake, and fruit-bearing trees will come. Take some of the feathers and throw them among the branches of the trees and birds will spring forth. Then throw the hair among the bushes on the ground and animals will be there."

He went to the king and said, "I have accomplished what you asked me." The king was much pleased, but now he said to him, "You and your wife have the power to show me hell, and would you please to do it." The violinist pondered the question and said, "Give me some time to think about it," but really he wanted to ask his wife what to do.

So when she got the chance she said to him, "You know that golden chain we brought from my father. Well, you take that and drag it up and down the mountain a few times and the door will open and the king can see hell. It looks like a mighty fine place but it is a very terrible place to go to. You do that, and when you have fixed it so that it can be seen, you tell him you want to give it to him as a gift. Make smaller chains of the golden chain you have to fasten the door and keep it open."

Then they took the king to see this fine place, and he and his servants passed through the iron door to see the beautiful temple. Then the fiddler jerked the chains loose and shut the door so that the king and all his people fell into hell. So the fiddler got his wife back again and they ruled the kingdom forever afterwards.

THIRTY

How the Sacred Duck Got His Yellow Breast

When life ends you may arise and have peace with Droma, but nevertheless it's a great calamity when the rock rolls down the mountain and takes your life.

Tibetan Proverb.

ONCE upon a time, on the top of a mountain which was quite flat and covered with grass and flowers, a frog and a rabbit were playing around, having a good time. In the midst of their fun, they found a beautiful golden pot. The frog exclaimed, "See what I have found. It's all mine! What a lot of money I shall have."

The rabbit said angrily, "It's mine, I saw it first."

And soon they were fighting fiercely. But all at once the rabbit stopped and remarked, "This won't do, let's go to the foot of the mountain and race back to the top, and the one that gets here first and gets in the pot shall have it, to-morrow to be the day of the race."

The rabbit was sure of success because he knew he could run and was certain the frog couldn't. The frog knew well enough he couldn't possibly win in that kind of race, so he thought of a scheme. He found two of his friends exactly like himself in every way. One, he took to the top of the mountain and put in the pot, the other he placed half way down the mountain, and located himself at the base. When the rabbit came next morning and they were ready to start on the race, the frog gave a few hops while the rabbit skipped on ahead. Much to his astonishment, when he got half way up the mountain, there was the frog hopping wildly along in front of him. He said to himself, "I must do better than this," and away he flew like the wind. But on reaching the summit there sat the frog in the pot. The rabbit had lost the race and also the gold.

Now, the frog didn't know how to get that big pot down the mountain, and while he was puzzling over it, a big duck, very dark in color, with mouse-colored breast, flew over him, stopped a minute, and asked his trouble. The frog told him what was the matter and asked if he could carry the pot to the bottom of the mountain. The duck said he could and would do so if he might have half. As there was nothing else to be done, the frog agreed and the duck carried it down for him, so there it was divided and the duck thought it was so beautiful that he took his half and smeared it on his breast, and that's where the sacred duck got his beautiful golden breast.

Note: On the tops of the mountains in Tibet and near the lakes are found these beautiful ducks.

A BIG DUCK, VERY DARK IN COLOR, FLYING OVER, STOPPED A MINUTE AND ASKED OF THE FROG HIS TROUBLE.

They are very tame and have no fear of people, as they are held to be sacred by the Tibetans, who believe them to be a reincarnation of some holy man because of the beautiful yellow color, which is their sacred color.

THIRTY-ONE

The Two Little Cats *

An arrow aimed straight will find the heart of your foe. But if you have no foe it does not matter about the arrow.

Tibetan Proverb.

IN the early, early days a very long time ago, there were two little cats going after some salt to put in their butter tea, for you must know that little cats in the early days didn't drink tea without salt. As they trotted along they met a Handre, and a Handre is the worst thing you could meet anywhere, for he has great big teeth that he crunches up little folks with, and horrid big eyes and clawlike hands and feet, so they were very much frightened and ran on faster than ever until they met a cow and the cow said, "Where are you going so fast, little cats?" and they answered, "Oh, we just met a Handre and he is going to come to our house and eat us up." "Never mind," said the cow, "I'll go with you and help protect you from the Handre." So they all ran on together. Soon they met a dog and he asked, "Where are you all going?" and the little cats said, "We are running away from the Handre." "Never mind," said the

* Told to me by little Lora MacLeod, now age six, who had been out of Tibet for about eight months.

dog, "I'll go with you and help protect you." They ran on and met a crow, and he said, "Stop a minute and tell me where you are going so fast." "Oh, we are running away home as fast as we can," said the little cats, "for the Handre is coming to eat us." Then they met a panful of ashes and it said, "Wait a minute and take me with you, for I can help too." Then they found a package of 100 needles, who asked if they might go and help against the Handre. Then a snake all curled up by the side of the road called out, "Where are you going, little cats?" "Oh, we are running home as fast as we can because the Handre is coming." And the snake said, "Take me along and I'll bite the Handre." As they trotted along they saw on a bench a little bowl of hard black peas. "Where are you going so fast, little cats?" asked the peas. "Oh, we are running home as fast as we can, for the Handre is coming." "Take me with you, little cats, and I'll help protect you from the Handre." So in front of their gowns they took the bowl of peas and all together soon came home. The cow they placed by the stair steps, the dog by the doorway, the peas on the stair steps, the crow in the water kang and the snake in the bread trough, the 100 needles in the bed and the pan of ashes on the ceiling and the little cats hid behind the door.

Soon the Handre came, I presume he flew in at the window, and he thought he would like to have a drink of water and when he went to get it the crow nipped him good and hard. Then he thought he would make some bread, and when he went to the bread tray the snake gave him a bite. Then he thought he would go upstairs and lie down on the bed and the needles stuck him dreadfully. He was getting madder and madder. He looked up to the ceiling to see if the little cats were hiding up there and the ashes spilled on him and filled his eyes full. Then he started to run down the stairs and he stepped on those hard peas and they hurt his feet dreadfully. Then he fell on the horns of the cow and she tossed him to the dog, who ate him up immediately, and the little cats came out from behind their door and had their supper in peace.

THIRTY-TWO

Story of a Juggler's Tricks

If you fight in the morning do not talk about it in the evening.

Tibetan Proverb.

ONCE upon a time, in a great city, lived a king who ruled over many, many people. In this city dwelt a powerful juggler who could make them cry or laugh, at his will. The king sent for him one day and said, "I have heard you can do wonderful things, that there is nothing beyond your ability [though he doubted it], and I want you to change my heart."

"Oh," said the juggler, "I have done this to the people, but I don't dare do this to you."

The king said, "You need not fear, just so you do not make me poor for the rest of my life. I will give you a paper agreeing not to punish you if you so wish." So he gave the paper to the juggler, returned to his home and forgot he had given such a promise.

One day the king heard that in his big hay field on the side of the mountain were a lot of people with horses and cattle, that there were all classes of men cutting his grass, and he had not given them permission to do so.

He called one of his head-men and said, "There

are a lot of people cutting my grass and I want you to go and see who it is and what they are doing it for, without my consent." The head-man went, and when he arrived at the field saw a golden throne, a silver throne, servants and men and so much grandeur that he was afraid to ask the ones in command what it all meant, so slipped around and asked a servant who these grand people were and what they were doing. The servant said that they were the king and his son of the lower regions, and the reason he was there now was because he was on his way up to heaven and had just stopped on the road. The head-man returned and reported to the king, who said, "Well, if this is the king of the lower regions I must go and take him some gifts." So he got his presents ready, went and presented them and asked, "If you are the king of the lower regions, why are you come to earth?" The king of the lower regions answered, "I am dwelling in the dark and live where the roots of the fig trees grow; the top is in the light where the gods partake of the fruit, while I am the owner of the trees and tend to the roots and make the trees produce the fruit, but I never get any of it. So I am going up to ask the gods about it."

The king of men on earth said, "I am glad you have come, we used to be neighbors and exchange gifts; in fact, we are somewhat related. I have a very nice daughter and you have your son, let me have him as a husband for my daughter."

The king of the lower regions answered, "I

have only three sons and this is the youngest, and I am much pleased with him and love him very much, but if you want him for your daughter, I will give him to you, as heretofore there has been a custom of this kind between kings such as we."

So he gave him his son and said, "I am going up to heaven now to see what the gods are going to do about all this fruit, and you watch the heavens and see whether we have any trouble or not."

The king of men took the son and returned to his palace, and in two or three days began to watch the skies. The heavens in a little while became as black as iron, dead men and hands and arms and legs and heads began to fall. He exclaimed, "Ah, I guess they are fighting sure enough."

One day a head that looked exactly like the king of the lower regions fell down, so he was quite sure that it was the king's head, and he thought he had better take it and burn it before his son-in-law found it, because he would be grieved. So he went off to burn it and his son-in-law saw the fire, and, calling one of the servants, who was a half-witted girl, asked what the big fire meant and all that smoke. She said, "Oh, you know your father's head fell down from heaven some time ago and they are burning it now."

When the son heard this, he gave a great cry and tried to rush to the fire, but they held him, though he finally broke away and ran and threw himself in the flames and perished.

In a few days here came the king himself down from heaven, for it had not been his head at all that had fallen. He went to camp in the same place in the hay field, where the king of men went to see him again and asked how the fight had ended. He answered, "We fought a little while, but one of the older gods intervened and fixed it up between us. They have acknowledged my right to part of the fruit, as the roots of the trees are in my kingdom. Why did not you bring my son out with you to see me?"

And the king of men said, "Well, dead men and a lot of things fell down from the sky and a head just like yours fell on top of my palace, and we took it and burned it. When your son found it out he ran and jumped in the fire and killed himself."

When the king of the lower regions heard this his face grew black as thunder and he said fearfully, "I am not dead, my body is here, and you are responsible for my son, and your life must pay for his life." The king of earth fell on his knees and began to beg for his life, saying, "I will give my kingdom, all my land and gold and all I have, if you do not ask me to pay my life for your son's life." So he yielded up all his goods until he had nothing left and kotowed over and over again.

"Well," said the king of the lower regions, "you need not kotow any more, just look up." When he looked, nothing was there but the old juggler sitting on a bench smiling at him.

The king was as angry as he could be when he

saw him, knowing he had been the victim of a trick, but remembered he had given the juggler a letter promising not to punish him for anything he would do. He swallowed his anger as best he could, took his servants and went back into his palace.

THIRTY-THREE

How the Wolf, the Fox and the Rabbit Committed a Crime

When an evil man gets mad at his enemy he beats his horse on the head.

Tibetan Proverb.

ONCE upon a time a wolf, a fox and a rabbit were walking along the road together when they met a wizard carrying a pack on his back. The rabbit said to the rest of them, "I'll go limping along in front of this fellow and he will put his load down and try to catch me, and you two slip around behind him, and when he puts his things down, you get them."

Sure enough, the man put his pack down, picked up some rocks and started after the rabbit in hot haste, while the wolf and the fox got his load and ran off with it. He came back pretty soon, when he found he couldn't catch the rabbit, and found his things were all gone. In great grief he started down the road, wondering what he would do and how he was going to live.

Meanwhile the wolf, the fox and the rabbit met in a chosen place and opened the pack to see what was in it. There were a pair of Tibetan boots with many layers in the soles, which made them very heavy, a cymbal with a tongue or clapper, an idol of tsamba and some bread. The rabbit acted as divider and said to the wolf, "You have to walk a lot, so you take the heavy boots." And the wolf took the boots. To the fox he said, "You have a lot of children, you take the bell for them to play with, and I'll take the food." The wolf put on the boots and started out to hunt a sheep. The boots were so heavy he fell on the ice and couldn't get up, and the shepherd found him and killed him. The fox took the bell and went in to his children ringing it, Da lang, da lang, da lang, and thought it would please them, but instead it scared them all to death. So the rabbit ate up the idol of tsamba and all the bread and got the best of that bargain.

THIRTY-FOUR

The Pewter Vase

If good words come—listen. If good food—eat.
Tibetan Proverb.

ONCE upon a time there were two men who were friends. They went out one day for a fine time together, and as they were walking around on the top of the mountain, they found a golden vase. One of them began to scheme in his heart how he could get it away from the other; but the other chap, who was a good fellow, proposed (as it did not cost anything) that they take and divide it and use the money for charitable purposes, giving it to the poor and to the lamas.

The first one said he didn't believe it was a real vase, that it was only an imaginary one, and that the gods had made it appear real to them. It was only an illusion. If they attempted to do anything with it, it would vanish entirely. They discussed the matter for a while and finally went down to the home of the man who desired it all for himself.

After a while he said to his friend, "You leave this vase here with me for a while; you want to go home now, and when you return we will divide it, each take his half and use it as he desires."

So the man went on to his home, remaining

there for three or four days. When he came back he met the man who had taken care of the vase and he was crying and beating his breast and tearing his hair. He exclaimed, "What is the matter with you and why are you carrying on in this manner?"

He replied, "Oh, I dare not tell you, it is too dreadful." But his friend said, "Tell me what it is, perhaps I can help you." For a long time he refused, but was finally persuaded and told him the trouble. "You know that golden vase we found, well, when I cut it it was only pewter." His friend replied, "That does not matter, we did not pay anything for it, we only found it, so we have lost nothing." Then the man stopped crying and felt wonderfully well satisfied with himself, thinking his friend had given up very easily and now he could keep the vase all for himself.

So the good man started home, but as he was leaving he said, "Your place here on the mountain is not a very pleasant spot, here it is cold and damp, while my place is fresh and green and warm, with plenty of grass for the cattle and fruit in abundance. You have two sons, let them take your cattle, go home with me and stay for a while." The man agreed and said it would be a nice trip for the boys, so they were allowed to accompany the good man. On the road as they were going home they saw two monkeys and caught them, taking them along. The man began to teach the monkeys tricks, taught them to dance when he sang for them, to come when he called them by name, and gave to them the names of his friend's two sons.

In a month or two he got a letter from his friend saying he was coming down for his boys. When he arrived he found the man crying and beating his breast and going on in a terrible manner. (Just before the arrival of the boy's father, he had taken the two boys and tied them up tight in a cave on the mountain.) As his friend came in he said, "What is the matter?" "Oh, I don't dare tell you," he answered, and went on crying and beating his breast. But his friend insisted and said, "It does not matter, perhaps I can help you." He finally consented and told him, "Well, you know, those two boys of yours that came home with me have changed into monkeys. If you don't believe it, call them and see." He called his sons' names and the monkeys came to him at once. The father looked at them for a little while and remarked, "Well, you are a smarter man than I, that vase is gold all right. You bring out the boys and I will divide the vase with you." So their trouble was peacefully settled and they were friends forever afterward.

THIRTY-FIVE

A Rabbit Story

The voice of the wolf is a sign to the sheep.
Tibetan Proverb.

ONCE upon a time there were two neighbor families, one family composed of an old mother bear and her son and the other of an old mother rabbit and her son. The children kept the house while the two mothers went out to dig roots. The rabbit's claws were sharp and quick and she got the most. This made the old bear mad so she killed the rabbit and took the dead body and roots home, although she couldn't dig very many, as her claws were dull. The little rabbit waited and waited and could not understand why his mother didn't come home. Finally he slipped over to the old bear's house to see what he could discover. He peeped in and saw that the old bear was cooking his mother, and she and her son sat down and ate her all up. He felt dreadfully bad and began to think of revenge, and said to himself: "Some day I will get even with them."

One day the old mother bear went out to carry water, and while she was gone the little rabbit heated an arrow red hot and shot the little bear in the ear and killed him. Then he took his mother's sack which the old bear had stolen with the roots in it and carried it away with him. As he went up the mountain he met a tiger and said to him, "There is a bear coming after me, Mr. Tiger, won't you save me and find a place for me to hide?" "All right, you crawl in my ear and that bear will never find you."

The old mother bear returned, bringing her kang of water, and found her son dead. She said, "The young rabbit has done this. I shall follow him and kill him." So, going after the rabbit, she came upon the tiger and asked, "Have you seen a fellow with gray fur and long ears anywhere? If you don't tell me the truth I will kill you." The tiger answered, "Don't talk to me that way, for I could kill you without very much trouble." And the old bear went on. The rabbit sat there in the tiger's ear eating some of the roots he had in his sack and the tiger could hear him munching away, and asked: "What are you eating?" "My own eye-ball," he answered. The tiger said, "Give me one, they seem very good." The rabbit handed him a root, the tiger ate and said, "That's very good. Let's take my eye-balls out and eat them, and if I am blind, since I saved you from this bear, you will take care of me and lead me around, will you not?" The rabbit said, "I will do that all right." So he dug out the tiger's two eye-balls and handed him some roots to eat in place of them. Then he went on leading the tiger, who now was blind, right up to the side of a big steep cliff, where he told him to lie down and go to sleep. Then he built a big fire on the other side of the tiger, who got so hot that when he moved away he fell over the cliff and killed himself.

The rabbit now went to a shepherd and told him, "There is a dead tiger up there, you can go and cut him up." Then he went to the wolf and said, "The shepherd is gone and you can go kill some sheep." Then he went to the raven and said, "You can go and pick the little wolves' eyes out, as their mother is gone to kill a sheep." Now the rabbit had done so much harm he thought he had better run away. He went into a far country and I expect he still dwells there.

THIRTY-SIX

The Story of a Juggler

The traveler is delayed by the men who stop—to the incurable medicine is of no use.

Tibetan Proverb.

ONCE upon a time, in a mountainous country, there was located a big city, in which dwelt a king. He had under him in different parts of his kingdom several ministers. One day he sent word to them that they were to come to the city, so they left their homes and came at his bidding. As one of the head-men was returning home, a juggler who was his exact counterpart, passed along before him; he was dressed the same, his speech was the same, and in every particular he was as near his double as could be found. When he arrived at home all the servants thought their master had returned and showed him to his bedroom.

When the true master returned after finishing his business with the king and found this stranger in his rooms, he asked his servants who this was who had taken possession of his house. The juggler heard him say this and called out, "Who is that fellow or beggar out there claiming this is his house? Put him outside." Then the true man exclaimed, "Don't you know me? This is a juggler that has come into my home, and you are putting me, the real owner, out."

"What is the matter with you all?" the juggler said. "You get out of here, this house and servants are all mine. Put him outside, you know these things belong to me."

They quarreled and quarreled, but finally the true man was put outside and ran and told the king what had happened to him. They were both called before the king and there they were standing before him, alike as two peas. "Well," he said, "I can not tell one from the other. I can't tell who is the right man, but both of you sit down and write a list of things that are in the house." The true man sat down and began to write, but would stop and think and make additions, so that his list might be complete. In the meantime, the juggler created a third man whom he sent back to the house, and this third one was just like the two men, and he brought back a list written from the house as he saw it.

The king now said, "I'll now see who is the true man." In fact, the true man had forgotten to write some things, while the list made by the other man was much more complete. So the king said to the juggler, "Well, I think you are the right man;" and gave him the house and land. The true man was very angry and said, "Well, here I am a beggar with nothing at all." In a few days the juggler got tired of being a big man, went to the king and said, "I hope you won't be angry, but the other man is the right fellow. I took his place by juggling, and it is really all his."

The king was not angry, but was much pleased to meet him, as he had heard of such men but had never seen one before. He showed him many honors, while the other man was restored to his rightful property and home.

THIRTY-SEVEN

The Story of a Turquoise

Whether you love or hate him a dumb man cannot tell —whether a thing is dirty or clean a blind man cannot tell.

Tibetan Proverb.

ONCE upon a time, away in the midst of some high, high mountains, there was a mud house. In it dwelt an old father and mother and a son and daughter. As the custom is in that country they gave their daughter to a man for a wife and the son took two wives, bringing them both into the home, making five in the family. The son's wives were called the little and the big wife, the one he married first being the big one with the most authority.

Suddenly one day the mother and her son died, so the two daughters-in-law took things into their own hands and proceeded to make a slave of the old father, sending him out on the mountain every day to tend the cattle, and giving him nothing to eat but a little sour cheese and blood. They got this blood by tying a yak so he couldn't move and sticking a needle into the jugular vein, letting him bleed a few bowls full, then turning him loose, and the next day bleeding another. The blood coagulated and became jelly-like, so they sliced it, warmed, cooked and ate it. The poor old man was very bad off and was about to starve to death, when he decided he would send to his daughter and see if she would give him some food. So he went down to the road to see if he could find any one going to her home, and as he sat waiting he fell asleep.

A big caravan of merchants came along and called out, "Old man, why are you sleeping here in the road?" He wakened and asked where they were going and when they named the place where his daughter lived he asked them to take a message to her. "Tell her that her mother and brother are both dead, that I am very happy, for I am a shepherd with great power, and have cheese and dried blood to eat; that there is no other man so powerful as a shepherd. Sometimes I have a little wine to drink, but in making the wine I don't need to beat up any barley, as there are no bubbles on top." (His wine was only water.) The merchants traveled on, found his daughter and delivered the message. She asked what time they were going back, as she wanted to send a message to her father. When they were ready to return they went for her message. She had a very valuable turquoise, and she made a brick of mud, put the stone in its center and said, "Tell him if he wants to live well to keep this brick, that he mustn't sell it, but may use it to gain influence."

The old man watched eagerly every day for the return of the caravan. At last it came and delivered the message and the brick. He understood at once, and took the brick up on the mountain, broke it open and got the stone, then he went down to the home where his daughters-in-law ruled supreme and showed it to the big wife, saying, "See what my daughter sent me. I'm not going to sell it, and when I die I will give it to you." So she decided to feed him and clothe him well, for she thought, "He won't live long and I'll soon get it."

One day when the big wife was not there he showed it to the second wife and said, "Look what I have; now I don't want to give it to the big wife and I don't want to sell it, but when I die I want to give it to you." So she was greatly pleased and thought, "Well, the old man won't live long, I'll be good to him and feed him well." So they both vied with each other to see who could treat him the best, but neither knew why the other was doing it. One day he became very ill and thought he was about to die, so he hid the stone on a cross beam of the house, just above a big water tank. His daughters-in-law were not home. He called the servants and told one of them to go to his daughter with this message, "Tell her to come to see me, and if she has no horse to ride, tell her to ride a donkey, and if I am dead when she arrives there is a great treasure on the neck of a big dragon and its image appears in the sea."

Soon he died and his daughters-in-law looked through everything he had, but could not find the stone. So the big wife said they must have a lot of lamas and read prayers for his soul. One day his daughter came and asked if there was any last message from her father and they told her "Yes." He said, "Tell her that there is a treasure on the back of the dragon's neck and its image appears in the sea." She understood at once, and looking in the water tank saw the image of the turquoise, climbed up on the beam and got it, tucked it in her bosom and went home.

THIRTY-EIGHT

A Wise Idiot

If shortsighted you cannot see far, but with sharp ears you can hear far.

Tibetan Proverb.

A LONG time ago there lived a family of good lineage that had been very rich, but had grown poor. In the same place also was a family who had been very poor but now was rich. Two women, one the wife of the former rich man and the other the wife of the present rich man, met one day in a temple where they had gone to worship. The rich woman said to the poor one, "Yes, we are rich, but everybody says our ancestors are bad or that we have none at all. Now you are poor, but your ancestors are fine, so let me have your son for my daughter." The poor woman said, "All right, you can have him." Her son had been very bright, but now he was going crazy. The rich people found out about the son's condition and without telling the poor family, secured a son from another family, whom their daughter married.

When the poor people saw this they were very angry with their son and said, "If you had any sense you would have gone to that rich family, but now, half idiot as you are, nobody wants you."

The son said, "Do not blame me, for if my ancestors had been all right, I would have been all right. It is their sins being visited upon me."

His father and mother gave him four gold pieces and told him to go away to a distant city and see if he could not improve.

As he journeyed along the road a shepherd was walking before him, and before the shepherd tripped a little bird, singing very sweetly. As soon as the shepherd came close to him he stopped singing and the shepherd said to him, "Your voice is very sweet, but why do you stop singing when I come near?"

The half idiot walking behind the shepherd now came up and said, "Teach me to say what you said to that bird and I will give you a gold piece." So he taught him, and the boy gave him one of his gold pieces and went on. Soon he heard a hunter say to a fox, "You have nice fur, and some day I will kill you and get it." So the idiot said to the hunter, "You teach me to say what you said to the fox and I will give you a gold piece." They talked a while and he taught him how to say it, and the boy gave up another of his gold pieces to the hunter.

Now this fool went on until he came to a place where there were two bridges, one made of one log, the other of two logs, and here were two men talking. One said to the other, "Let's run a race over these bridges. I'll run over the one log, as it is shorter, and will be quicker, you run over the other built of two logs."

The silly fellow heard them, came up and said, "Teach me what you have been saying and I will give you a gold piece." So they taught him and he parted with another piece of his money.

He went on and saw two fellows fighting, and one of them said, "If you don't behave I'll send you to the official." The fool asked to be taught that, and parted with his last gold piece.

Now, since his money was all gone, he decided to return to his own country. When he reached home, they were celebrating the wedding of the rich girl and her husband and the fool mixed with the crowd. The girl saw him and said, "It won't do for me to go out, it will make him sad to see me." But he saw her anyway, and as he had learned only four sentences he began to say the first one to her thus: "You're a nice bird and your voice is beautiful. Why did you stop singing when I came near?"

She went into the house and said to her parents, "You know that half-witted fellow to whom you were going to marry me? Well, he is pretty sharp, I can tell you." So they told her to bring him up to the top of the house and they would at least give him something good to eat.

Then he said his next sentence, "You she-fox, you've got mighty nice hair, and some day you will fall into my hands." The bride ran and told her father and mother, "Oh, he was awfully fierce, you should have heard what he said to me."

After a while, when they were all eating, there were not enough chopsticks to go round, so this fool got only one, but he ate his food quickly and said his third sentence, "When there are two bridges, one of one log and one of two logs, go over the one-log bridge, it is always the quickest." The girl told her father and mother this and they concluded he wasn't a fool at all. So when the guests were all gone and this man still remained, he said his last sentence, "If you treat me like this, I am going to take you to the official." "This will never do, to have him take you to the official. He hasn't said much to-day, but it has all been mighty smart; so we will give this other man a lot of money and send him back home, and keep this man for your husband."

THIRTY-NINE

The Man and the Monkeys

The male deer from the top of the hill can see afar off. But the goose on her nest thinks only of the egg she covers.

Tibetan Proverb.

ONCE upon a time when the garden of Eden was in the world, a man traveling around the country found the garden and went in through the gateway. He thought it a very beautiful place. There was everything good to eat, cakes and candies and fruits of all kinds. He said to himself, "Here I'll stay. I won't have to work any more, for everything I need is here, so here I'll remain." He thought he would take a nap, and crawled up one of the big trees and went to sleep among the branches. But he slept too soundly and forgot he was up the tree, and went to turn over and tumbled into a lake. One of the monkeys in the forest saw him fall into the water and tried in every way to help him out, and finally said, "I'm too little. I can't pull you out, but if I can grow big and strong I'll be able to help you out." So he began to exercise every day by picking up small stones, and then every day a little larger one, until finally he grew strong enough to lift a big stone, and so was able to get the man out of the water. After the man was rescued he didn't feel very well and the monkey proposed that he exercise a while with the stones. He threw the stones about a while until he felt quite warm, then thought he'd go to sleep again, but this time he'd lie down on the ground. The monkeys were all in the trees talking and chattering, so he didn't sleep very soundly. When he roused up he thought, "This is a beautiful place if there just wasn't so many monkeys." (I guess he forgot how much one of them had just helped him.) "If these monkeys would all die, I'd go home and get my family and stay here, because we wouldn't have to work at all."

By this time it was evening and the monkeys were all asleep in the trees. So he shook all the trees until the monkeys fell out on the ground and were killed by the fall. Then, quite well satisfied with himself, he started home to bring his family back to the garden to live. But on the way the monkey god, who looks after monkeys, good and bad, and knew the man had been mean to the monkeys when they had been kind to him, turned himself into a big snake, met him on the path and swallowed him.

ONE OF THE MONKEYS SAW HIM FALL INTO THE WATER AND HASTENED TO HELP HIM OUT.

FORTY

The Story of the Tree of Life

If you do not quarrel you are safe—if you have no debts you will be rich.

Tibetan Proverb.

ONCE upon a time there was an old beggar dressed in rags and tatters, with wisps of gray hair about his face. He was so very old that it seemed he could have never been young, and never in all his life had he had a bath. This old beggar traveled everywhere asking for rice and tsamba and receiving more rice than he could eat he spread it out in the sun to dry and went on begging.

One day as his rice was drying a hundred parrots came along and ate it all up. When he came home he was angry and said, "Here I work every day, begging for a little food, and these old parrots come along and eat it all up." So he planned to be revenged and made one hundred snares of bamboo, put them all around in the reeds and went off to beg again. When he returned, sure enough, he had caught the whole hundred in his snares. Among them happened to be the king of the parrots, who, before the old man came home, spoke to his companions, saying: "We are in a bad fix. He has caught us all and he'll kill us every one. When we see him coming let us all hang down as though we are dead, then he will take us out of the snares and pitch us away. But the first one thrown must keep count, and as soon as one hundred are thrown he shall call out and we will all fly away. We must all lie perfectly still until the last one is thrown."

Finally the old man came home with some rocks in the front of his gown to throw at the parrots, for he didn't think they would all be dead, but when he saw them all hanging perfectly still he climbed up and began to throw them down. He had pitched down ninety-nine and was untying the string off the king's leg when the rocks in his gown got in his way and he threw one of them down. As soon as it lit, away flew the ninety-nine.

"Huh, they were all fooling me, but I have one left and I'll take a rock and kill him." The parrot suddenly came to life and sticking up his thumb said, "Please don't kill me, it is true we were very bad and did eat up your rice, but you are a good man, so don't kill me, take me and sell me and you can get more than your price of the rice."

So he tied a string around the parrot's leg, took him to town and tried to sell him to a merchant. The beggar said he was a fine parrot and could talk, but he didn't know what he was worth, so the merchant had better ask the parrot himself. The parrot answered that he was worth a lot of money and the merchant must pay the old man fifty taels of silver for him. The merchant gave the money to the old man, who almost died of joy to have so much money.

After the parrot had been with the merchant for two or three years he asked permission to visit his home and parents, as they were getting old. He said, "You treat me very nicely here and I love you, and I will soon come back again and bring you some nice fruit."

The merchant took the chain off the parrot's leg and let him go. He was gone two or three months, when one day he came, carrying some seeds in his mouth, and said, "Plant these seeds, and when you are old and eat of the fruit of this tree you will be young again. Plant the seed carefully, and in three years you will have plenty of fruit." The merchant planted the seeds and at the end of three years, sure enough, there was much fruit. One day he was in his garden and one of the fruits had fallen to the ground, but he was afraid to eat it lest the parrot had thought of this as a scheme to kill him. That night a poisonous snake coiled around the fruit and slept. The next morning the merchant called his dog and showed him the fruit, which he ate, and which killed him immediately. The merchant knew now that the parrot had schemed to kill him, and poured hot water on him and scalded him to death.

Now in this country were two old people, very frail and too feeble to go out and beg, so they were about to starve to death. So the old man said one day, "Let's eat some of this fruit; if it makes us young it's all right, if it poisons and kills us, it doesn't matter, as we are about to die anyway." So they got their walking sticks and went slowly to the merchant and asked him for some of the fruit. He said, "You can't eat that, for it will kill you at once." They told him it didn't matter, for they were about to starve to death anyway, and it was easier to take poison and die quickly. He finally gave them one each, they ate it and grew young at once. They were much pleased and almost worshiped the man. Then the merchant knew that something must have poisoned the fruit as it lay on the ground and he was grieved to think that he had killed his parrot.

FORTY-ONE

The Story of the Man with the Goitre

A man without wickedness needs no punishment—without an ax no tree can be cut down.

Tibetan Proverb.

A LONG time ago, in a lonely country among the mountains, there lived a man with a big goitre on his neck, and he owned a cow. One day the cow wandered away. The man went out to find her, but had to go so far from home that he could not get back that night. Looking around he found two caves, one big one and one little one, and decided to spend the night in the little one.

As he went in and sat down cross-legged on the ground, he began talking the affair over with himself, saying, "My cow is lost and I can not find her, and I have nothing to eat. I am far away from home and can't get back, and I have to stay out here, and I am very much afraid."

Now the big cave was the place where all the ghosts met, but in the small cave only one ghost had his home. This ghost went over to the big cave to the assembly of ghosts and told them there was a man in his cave. They told him to go back and bring him over to them and they would eat him, but he pleaded with them and said, "Please don't kill the man, for I am his landlord, and it wouldn't be good for me if you did so." He told them, too, that the man had a big goitre on his throat. Then they said to him, "Go and cut that goitre off his neck and bring it over here, and we will eat that."

"All right, that will do," he said, and slipped back into his own cave. He cut the goitre off and took it to them, but when they saw it they said it was too big, it wasn't fit to eat, and they left it in the cave. When the man wakened in the morning he had no goitre and was pleased as could be. He soon found his cow and started down the mountain.

When he got home without his goitre, another man who had one came and asked him how he got rid of his. He told all of his adventures and the mysterious disappearance of the thing. The other man thought he would do the same and get rid of his. He drove his cow up on the mountain and then went to find her, hid in a cave and talked to himself about the cow that was lost, saying that he could not find her and that he would have to stay there all night. The ghosts assembled again in the big cave and the one who dwelt in the small cave told them again he had a guest, and they of course wanted to eat him. But he begged them not to, saying that he would cut off the goitre and bring that over. "Pouf, who wants to eat goitre; we have already got one we don't like. Take that and stick it on the back of his neck." When the man wakened in the morning he thought something nice had happened to him, but when he felt his neck there was his goitre just the same; then the back of his neck felt queer and he put his hand there and found another one. Then he was very angry and took his cow and went home and never came out again where people could see him.

FORTY-TWO

The Story of the Beggar

An old man and a bat never grow old. But an old woman has to find comfort in the Juniper. (Juniper is burned to the gods.) *Tibetan Proverb.*

ONCE upon a time there was a beggar, with hair in twisted wisps, dirty, dirty face and hands and a few rags for clothing, who begged from the people of the village for his living. On one lucky day he had succeeded in begging about a bushel of barley. He took it home with him, put it in a sack and tied it up to the ceiling to the cross poles of his little hut, so the rats couldn't get it, and then lay down upon his bundle of rags to sleep. He began to count how rich he would be if he got a bushel of barley every day. He could afford him a wife. When he got a wife he would have a son, and he wondered and wondered what he should name his boy. Toward morning the light from the moon fell upon his bed and wakened him and gave him a brilliant thought. He would name his son Däwä Dräbä, which means the light of the moon; he was so pleased he jumped up from his bed, dancing around the room, flourishing his beggar's staff in his glee. But alas, he flourished it a bit too fiercely, for it struck his big bag of barley, which fell on him and killed him, and the father of Däwä Dräbä was dead.

FORTY-THREE

The Wily Poor Man

When the man is gone—the woman has no leader—when the rooster is dead the donkey has to bray.

Tibetan Proverb.

ONCE upon a time, in the center of a great wide plain in a mountainous country, was a Hläkäng in which was a statue of Chenrezik, the god with a thousand arms. Near the temple was a small house, and in this house lived two old people who had a daughter whose name was "Ceering Droma," which meant Golden Goddess of Mercy. The parents thought it was about time that the girl should marry, so they said to each other, "To-morrow we will go to the Hläkäng, take some gifts for the god, kotow before him and cast lots as we ask about her marriage."

About a half-day's journey away there lived a poor man who brought up peaches and walnuts to sell. He happened to be near the window and heard these old people talking about going to the temple; so the next day as soon as the doors were open, he slipped in and hid in the great god. The old people came, worshiping the god, and saying, "Great and merciful Chenrezik, we have many things and only one daughter, and as we are very old and may die and leave them, it's for you to tell us what is best to do. We leave it all in your hands. Is it better for our daughter to become a nun or to be married? When we lie down tonight to sleep will you speak to us in a dream or will you speak to us here, now? Help us to think aright and know your meaning."

The fellow that was hiding in the god spoke through his nostrils and said, "There will be a man come to you in the morning, you must give her to him."

The old people thought this was very wonderful that the god had really spoken and they could be in no doubt as to what he meant. After they were gone the man slipped out of the temple, and on the next morning early, there he was kneeling at the old people's door. The woman saw him and called to her husband, "Here he is, the god told us he would come." So she led him in, had him sit in the place of honor and put fine food before him. They gave him the daughter for his wife, gave him a handful of turquoise stones and asked him to be very kind to her. He said he would, and took his wife and his peach box and started home. As he neared home he began to think of the lies he had told the old people, saying he was rich and had a fine house and plenty to eat, and he knew there would be nothing to eat at all. So he thought he would go on ahead and see what could be done. He took his box off of his back, put his wife and the turquoises in it and set it down in the sand and covered it all up, then went home and borrowed all the things he could, good food, good cushions and rugs. He told his neighbors they must not tell he was poor, because that day he had gotten him a wife and she wasn't to know it. It took him about four or five days to get this done, and all this time his wife sat there in the box in the sand.

One day there were three kings going along the road with their servants, their bows and arrows and a tiger, all out for a good time. They thought they would stop and shoot at the mark. They aimed at the pile of sand, and, ping! the arrow hit the box. They dug the thing out and found the girl and the turquoises all covered up in the sand.

The king said, "Who are you?"

She answered, "I'm the daughter of the king of the lower regions."

The king said, "Will you be my wife?"

She said that she wouldn't mind, only somebody would have to sit in the box. He said that the tiger would do, so they put him in the box and covered it all with sand as she had been covered.

After her husband had fixed his house he stole down to where he had buried his box, dug it out and carried it home on his back. He thought, "This woman will be afraid of me by now. I'll open the box and see if she is ready to be obedient." (He had already told his neighbors that if they heard them fighting a little they needn't come over and interfere.) He fixed the bed ready for his wife, opened the box and the tiger jumped out at him, tore his clothes and nearly frightened him to death. He began to yell for his neighbors in a loud voice, but he had shut and locked the outside gate so that his wife couldn't get out if she tried to. His neighbors heard the noise and laughed saying he had just got a wife and they were already fighting. So they waited until the next morning to go over, and when they went in there sat a big tiger with his mouth all covered with blood. As soon as he saw them, he ran away into the forest, and all they could find was a few little bones.

In the meantime the girl had married a king and had much gold and riches. But the people in the kingdom and the head-men of the cities did not approve, and said, "This woman came out of the ground and has no lineage, and this, her son, who will be our king and rule over us, will have no ancestors." When the queen heard this murmuring she thought the best thing she could do was to go back to her father and mother and stay there, but decided to wait till the fifteenth, when the moon was full. So she ran away, and as she neared her home, or where her home used to be, she found in its place a palace, and where the old building had stood there was a great temple covered with golden minarets with bells everywhere, which rang sweetly when the wind blew. There was a man in her father's house, and she asked him whose house this was. He spoke her father's and mother's name, so she went into the house to rest. She found the lower story full of horses, mules and cows, and she knew these people must be very wealthy. When she got into the guest room there sat her father and mother on cushions and fine rugs. She bowed down before them and said, "I have come home. I'm so glad you are here and not dead, for all my husband's people say that I have no lineage and am not fit to be the mother of the future king. Now, if only they could come to see you and find out how rich and great you are they might change their minds."

Her father and mother said, "Tell them to come over and see us, if they don't believe you have parents and a rich home."

So they invited the king, who came with fifty of his head-men. They stayed about three days and were treated royally by the old couple, and changed their opinion when they saw her family and their wealth. The king and his men returned, and she said she would stay a few days longer with her father and mother. That night as she lay down to sleep she was cold and couldn't get warm, and as she had always had plenty of rugs and things, she couldn't understand it, and got up to see what was the matter. She was sleeping on the ground and her pillow was a rock, and she found when she got up that she had dreamed all of this, for she found her father and mother were nothing but bones. She had started to run away again, and falling asleep by the wayside dreamed all this about them. So she thought the best thing she could do was to go back to the king.

FORTY-FOUR

The Quarrel of the Five Friends

The mouth is the door of quarrels. To open it is easy—to close it difficult. The tongue is the foundation of quarrels—it is easy to use—difficult to keep it still.

Tibetan Proverb.

ONCE upon a time, when the world was young, there lived in a city the son of a rich man, the son of a painter, the son of a fortune teller, the son of a carpenter, the son of a doctor and the son of a silversmith. These six men were all close friends, so close that they planned they would run away together. They left their parents and traveled to another place, where they agreed they would separate for six years, each man going his own way, seeking adventure. At the end of that time they would all meet in the city of their birth. Before they separated each planted a soul tree, a tree that knew things. If one of the men was dead or was not prospering, his soul tree would tell of it. It was a custom in that land for each home to have a soul tree and to care for it and water it and protect it with a wall, if need be. When all was well the tree grew and flourished, if ill, it withered away or died. After six years, when they assembled, they were all to look at the trees and see if any were dying or withered, and if the man who owned the withered tree wasn't present, they would know he was not doing well and must hunt for him; or if the tree was dead they would know that the man was dead.

The son of the rich man went far away to a little house in a valley. He went to the door and asked for entrance and it was opened by a little old man and a little old woman, who lived there, who asked, "Son, who are you, whence have you come and where are you going?" He told them, "I have come from a far country and have come to see if you can give me something to eat."

The old people answered, "Well, we like the looks of you, and if you will stay and become the husband of our daughter, who is very handsome, we will be much pleased." He went in and sat down, and soon the daughter entered, and she was pretty, indeed. He sat thinking about his native land, how far he was from home, but finally concluded it would be the best thing he could do to marry the girl and stay there. She was glad to see him and asked about his home and his adventures, and fell in love with him at once; so they were married immediately.

Down below this little place there lived a king who had many servants. One afternoon, soon after the bride had been to bathe, the women all went down to the river to have a bath and found a beautiful ring which the bride had lost in the water. They took it to the king, who thought to himself, "No one but a fine woman would own such an exquisite ring as this." So he called a servant and told him to find the owner. The man went out, walked up the river until he came to the little house, where he saw the woman, saw how pretty she was and said, "This must be she." He wanted to take her at once to the king, but she refused to go, saying she had a husband. So the servant took them both before the king, as kings' laws must be obeyed. When he saw how beautiful she was he said she must be the daughter of a god. He became displeased with his wives, saying they were only dogs and hogs compared with her. He gave her gifts of gowns and jewels and wanted her to stay with him, but the girl was afraid and didn't want to stay, for she loved her husband. Knowing this the king decided he must get rid of him, so he called his servants and had them take the husband down to the river, dig a hole, kill him, put him in it, and cover the place with a rock.

Six years passed and the five men returned to look at their trees. All were there except one, and all the trees were flourishing except one, the tree of the son of the rich man being dead. They decided to find him, but though they hunted in every city in the world they could find no trace of him at all. One day the son of the fortune teller said, "Perhaps I had better tell his fortune and see what has become of him," and then he told this: "We will find his body in a hole on the bank of a river." They hunted and hunted many days and finally found the place, but the rock was so big that all five of them could not move or lift it. So the son of the silversmith chiseled it off and made it smaller until they could get it off the hole and they found him; then the son of the doctor gave him some medicine that brought him to life and he could talk.

They decided they would get his wife back for him, but it wouldn't do to go and demand her, as the king would kill all six of them at once; so the son of the carpenter said he had a scheme, he would make a flying machine. He made an affair with wings and a tail, which he called a wooden bird. This would go up and down and any place he wished. The son of the painter colored it with many beautiful colors. When it was all finished the son of the rich man got in it and sailed up toward heaven. He flew around and around and finally stood right over the king's palace. The people were all looking at the wonderful and beautiful bird sailing up above them, and the king said to his wife, "Take some nice food up there on the roof and maybe he will come down." So she took the food and went to the roof and the bird came closer and closer, down to the place where she stood. Finally the bird landed on the flat roof beside her and a man stepped out. She was pleased, knew him and said, "I thought you were dead, and I never expected to see you again."

"Are you really pleased," he asked her, "or would you rather stay with the king? Choose for yourself. Either go with me, getting into this wooden bird, or stay here. You need not fear the king if you go with me, for he never can catch us in this bird."

So she stepped into the machine and away they flew to where the five friends awaited them. They alighted, and when they saw her they, too, thought she was beautiful. The son of the rich man said, "I have been dead and brought to life again and now have my wife, and all this I owe to you."

He thanked them over and over, for all they had done. Then he said, "We will be so happy to live as man and wife again," and this made his friends very angry. The son of the fortune teller said, "Well, nobody would have known where you were if it had not been for me, and the girl by rights belongs to me." The son of the silversmith said, "Your business just telling where he was did not amount to anything, it was I that broke the rock away, and the girl should be mine." The son of the doctor said, "What's the use of all your work, just to find the corpse was nothing; it was I that brought him to life, and she should be mine." The son of the carpenter said, "It didn't do any good to bring him to life, it was I who made the wooden bird to get her in, and she belongs to me." The son of the painter said, "The machine was no good until I painted it to look like a bird, and the king sent his wife up, instead of a slave to feed it, so the woman should be my wife."

So they stood quarreling and quarreling until they saw a man coming along the road, and called him in to settle it. They told him about what each had done. He knew not how to answer, but told them this story,

"One time a lot of men owned a fine chorten,* and as they couldn't decide to whom it belonged they cut it into pieces and divided it." So these six men drew their knives and slew the girl.

* A chorten is a stupa, or pagoda, sometimes of gold, more often made of clay, of religious significance.

FORTY-FIVE

The Frugal Woman

If the yak is blind he will tumble off the road.
Tibetan Proverb.

ONCE upon a time, a long, long time ago, in a little mud village, lost somewhere now in the mountains of Tibet, lived a group of people. A tiny stream of water from underground, perhaps from a magic horse's head or a magic cow's head, flowed and never went dry. This stream gave them all the water they needed.

Ruling over this village was a chief whom they called the head-man of the village. He settled all their small quarrels, punished offenders and his word was law up to the matter of life and death. He had a very handsome son, who had no wife. The middleman had made a marriage, all sides agreeing, between this son and the daughter of a prince who ruled over a slightly bigger territory. This prince, with a hundred men and their musical instruments, dancers and singers, gifts for the family, milk money for the mother and wedding gifts of jewels to the bride, went down to claim his wife. The head-man feasted and kept them exchanging gifts for about three days, then they started to return, taking the bride witn them.

The mother followed her to the door, as she was leaving, and said, "Do not grieve because you are leaving home. In one month you can come back and visit us."

Her father and big brother and little sister all said, "Don't be sorry, for now you are the wife of this big prince, and will have plenty to eat and nice clothes to wear," and her mother said, "You must keep as clean as if you were looking in a mirror all the time. You must be good to your own servants and kind to your husband's parents, and also be charitable and give to the poor. You mustn't say bad things, as that's just as silly as a billy-goat trying to butt down a stone wall with his horns."

So they tried to comfort her as she went away weeping, and told her to be happy and contented.

Now the greater part of the caravan had gone on before and only she and a few of the maid servants were left behind. Those in advance went on and on and when night came, they stopped in a fine valley and prepared to camp for the night.

By and by when she came up to them she said, "This won't do. This is a bad place, for if it should rain everything, including ourselves, would be washed away."

She went on a little bit farther, found another spot and sent back word to them to come up there where she had stopped. As the loads were already off the yak and all was prepared for the night they were very angry because all the loads had to be tied on again, the ponies gathered in from where they were grazing, and only to go such a little distance!

They said to one another, "This woman is unspeakable. She comes from a very common home, but now she is the wife of this prince she thinks she can make us do as she likes." So grumbling a great deal, they unloaded and made camp again for the night. But sure enough that night a big rain came and washed everything out of the valley where they had first stopped. When they saw that they said, "If we had been there everything would have been lost and we would have been dead. She is a prophetess and knows all things. We owe our lives to her."

So they journeyed on and came to her husband's home, where they feasted again for three days. Now it was time for the servants her father had sent with her to return. She gave them all gifts, told them good-by and sent them back to her father's house.

Now some of her husband's servants had heard her mother tell her she was to keep as clean as if she were looking in a mirror all the time. So they went to the prince and asked him what it meant, that they didn't understand that saying at all. When she got up in the morning, she swept the house and combed her hair and saw that everybody had food before she would eat anything. One day her husband said to her, "What did your mother mean by that saying?"

She answered, "My mother's meaning was this: that I wasn't to be greedy and eat good things all

ONE DAY A BIG CRANE FLYING OVER THE PALACE, CARRYING A FEW HEADS OF RICE FOR HIS OWN FOOD, DROPPED SOME GRAINS INTO THE PALACE GARDEN.

the time, but if I waited on others I'd be hungry and things would taste good to me. And looking in the looking glass meant I was to keep myself clean and the house clean so I'd never be ashamed of it."

One day a big crane coming from near the sea was carrying a few heads of rice for his own food; as he flew over the palace, he dropped a few of the grains, which the servants gathered up and took to the mistress of the house. She said to them, "We must plant a few of these seeds and be careful with them, for they make fine medicine for fevers."

They divided the grains among the different families, who took them home and planted them. After a while the king's wife took sick with the fever and he called all his chief head-men of the surrounding villages and all the lamas, who told him that if she didn't have some rice from near the sea she would die. Then he sent out to all the people he knew, asking if they had any rice, but none of them had a grain. Finally he sent to this woman, the wife of the prince, and asked if she had any rice, and she said, "Of course I have. Not only for her but for all the sick people in the country."

So she sent some to the king's wife, who got well, and she gave it also to all the other sick folks, and from this time on the people worshiped her and always went to her in times of trouble.

FORTY-SIX

The Story of Yugpacan, the Brahman. From Jaschke

In a narrow road it is difficult to stop and talk. Call upon the gods—on the plains is the time to sing and be happy.

Tibetan Proverb.

ONCE upon a time there was a farmer. One day one of his neighbors named Yugpacan borrowed his bull. He took the animal and in a few days returned it and left it loose in the owner's yard while the owner was eating, and the bull ran away. When the owner had finished his meal he went to his neighbor and asked for the bull. Yugpacan replied, "I turned him into your yard." The owner said, "You have lost my bull." So they had a quarrel and both started for the official to have the matter settled.

As they went along they met a man whose horse had gotten loose and was running away, and he called to these two to head him off and catch him. Yugpacan picked up a stone and threw it at the horse and killed him. Then the owner said, "Now you have slain my horse, come with me to the official and he will settle the matter." They all started on and came to a wall and Yugpacan jumped over the wall and fell on top of a gardener who was digging in his yard and killed him. His wife came running up and said, "You have murdered my husband and must make good." Yugpacan answered, "I can't pay you for your husband." "Well," she said, "come with me to the official and he will make you pay."

They all started along again and came to the bank of a river where they saw a carpenter swimming across holding a small ax in his mouth. Yugpacan ran to the brink of the river and asked him a question, whereupon the swimmer opened his mouth to answer it and straightway dropped the ax into the water. The carpenter was angry and said, "You must pay me for my ax." Yugpacan said, "I won't pay you." "All right then, come with me to the official and we will see about that."

The whole crowd in due time came to the great man who was to decide their cases. He asked, "What is the matter that you have come to me?" The farmer and Yugpacan proceeded at once to tell their case; then the official said to Yugpacan, "You returned the bull, but the owner didn't see it, and as you didn't say anything I will cut off your tongue." Then he said to the owner, "Because you didn't see it, I will take out one of your eyes." So he settled the first case, saying, "The man who has a tongue should be able to talk, and the man with eyes should be able to see."

The man whose horse had been killed now stated his case. The official turned to Yugpacan and asked how he had killed the horse. "Well," he answered, "he asked me to help catch his horse and I picked up a rock and threw it at the horse." Then he asked the owner of the horse, "Why did you ask him to head off your horse? My decision is this, because you, Yugpacan, threw and killed the animal, I will cut off one of your hands." Then to the owner of the horse, "Because you told him to help catch your horse I will cut off your tongue." Thus ends the second case.

The woman now presented her case and said that Yugpacan had killed her husband. Yugpacan said he was just on top of the wall and fell off and did not see the gardener and landed on him. The official decided, "Well, you have killed this man, so to make it good you must be this woman's husband."

The carpenter now said, "Yugpacan, while I was in the water, asked me a question, and as I opened my mouth to answer my ax dropped and was lost in the water." The official said, "Because you carried your ax in your mouth instead of your hand I will knock out two of your teeth, and Yugpacan, because he asked you a question while you were swimming, I will cut off another slice of his tongue."

Each one then begged the official to forgive Yugpacan for all his wickedness, and forgive each of them and leave them each as they were in the first place, which he very obligingly did.

FORTY-SEVEN

The Story of Da Jang. From Amundsen

In life there are just two things—happiness and misery. One you say and the other you think.

Tibetan Proverb.

IN a large city in a distant land called Nyen Yo lived a man, Da Jang, who was a very skillful juggler. He had a friend named Pelzang, who had a wife and daughter. One day Da Jang said to Pelzang, "You should learn to be a juggler; it might be of use to you some time." Pelzang answered, "What is the use of that, a horse would mean much more to me." Da Jang, displeased with the reply, went away muttering that some day he would prove to his friend that juggling was useful.

A few days later, after Pelzang had eaten breakfast and was outside the cottage spinning yarn, while his wife was washing up the wooden bowls on the inside of the house, Da Jang arrived riding on a phantom horse.

"Friend Pelzang," he said, "buy this horse."

Pelzang replied, "I have nothing to buy it with, I do not want it."

But Da Jang said, "It is a fine horse with a fine trot, and if you will buy it I will let it go cheaply. Mount and try it," he urged.

"Well," Pelzang said, "if you will let it go cheap enough I will take it," and he got on the horse, which set off in a wild gallop beyond control. By sunset he had arrived in an unknown place, and he looked all around and finally saw a house from which smoke was rising, and went to the door and knocked. An old lady came out. She might be a demon, thought the man, but there was no place else to go. He asked for lodging and bed from the old lady. "Come in," she said. He entered and found she had three daughters. Having given him delicious food and drink, the old lady inquired, "Who brought you here?" He explained that his horse had run away and landed him in this strange place. She then proceeded to say, "Now, you have nowhere to go, and moreover, this is a small place without a ruler, so say no more, stay with me and be husband to one of the girls and landlord to this place. Even if you leave here you will not get anywhere." He thought there was nothing else to do, as his horse had entirely disappeared, so he decided to remain, and took one of the daughters for his wife, and in a few years had two sons and one daughter.

One day, the mother having gone to get some wood, the children were playing by the river. It was evening and the moon shone into the water. One boy, trying to catch it, fell in and was carried off by the current. As the father tried to rescue him, the other boy fell into the river in his excitement, and both slipped away and were gone. While thus fruitlessly occupied a tiger came and carried off the girl from the bank. The father uttered a cry and fell down almost dead with terror and grief. His wife, in the meantime, finding out what had happened, jumped into the river also.

"What an unfortunate creature I am." Tearing out the hair of his head, behold, it had turned white. He thought it would be better for him to die too, so he sprang into the water. He could not sink, but, strange to say, seemed to be lying on the ground, and as he looked up, behold he was back at his own house door. He went in and heard his wife singing, and then he told her what had happened to him and she said, "Are you demented or bewitched? Something has happened to you; I have just finished washing the bowls."

He went outside and, sure enough, there was the yarn in its place just as he had had it, and looking at his wife she was no older in appearance nor was the baby any bigger, and looking at himself in the mirror, his hair was as black as before. As nothing was changed he understood that the juggler had played a trick on him.

Moral: The affairs of this world are like the delusions of the juggler.

FORTY-EIGHT

Like unto Solomon. From Jaschke

Women have 6 faults—1st, when her legs are long she will fall down; 2nd, when they are short she will stand up; 3rd, when she is fat she will run; 4th, when her face is red she will cry; 5th, when her face is black she will get angry; 6th, when her mouth is big she will laugh.

Tibetan Proverb.

ONCE upon a time two women were quarreling over one boy, trying to decide to which one he belonged. They could not settle the case, so they took it before the king of the land, who, being wise and of great understanding, thus ordered: "One of you take hold of the right hand of the boy and the other of the left hand and pull, the one who gets him may carry him off."

When he had so spoken, she, who was not the boy's mother, because she had no love for him, and not caring whether she hurt him or not, pulled with all the force she had. She, who in truth was the boy's mother, because she loved him, and fearing she might hurt him, though she was the stronger of the two, did not pull very hard. Then the king said to her who had pulled very hard, "He is not your son, but belongs to the other woman," to whom he gave the boy, who at once happily carried him away.

FORTY-NINE

Tibetan Song

TRANSLATED FROM TIBETAN BY

A. L. SHELTON, M.D.

1.

In the middle of the sea is a high mountain.
The sun is shining on the mountain, on a great plain
The flowers are blooming.
When the sun is shining on the yellow flowers
All men are pleased.
On the mountain are grass and water.
The cows are resting in the grass, water and sun.
On this mountain the evergreens grow always.
The cuckoos are resting in the trees.
The trees are blue, cuckoos are blue, all men are happy.

2.

The snows are everlasting.
There are small and large black tents.
All the lions are tied.
Milk is as the waters of the sea.
The tents are like cliffs.
All the eagles are tied.
Milk is like the sea.
On the plain are the tents great and small.
The deer are all tied.
Their milk is as the sea.

3.

At the head of this great plain
Are ninety-nine hundred fine horses.
Their saddles are all of gold.
The name of this is beautiful. (All immortals live here.)
In the middle of this plain
Are many herds of cattle.
They all eat from golden stalls.
They are immortal.
At the lower end of this plain, the sheep are herded.
They are all happy and immortal.

TIBETAN MUSIC

Recorded by Ray Howard Crittenden
as played by Dorothy Shelton with the Tibetan instrument, the "Fuchin." First recorded notes of these tunes, 1921.

1.

"Rigung du tsuk"

2.

"A-ru-leh"

3.

"Dorgiling ba"